Ralph Creger, seated above, is chief train dispatcher for the Arkansas division of the Rock Island Railroad. He was born in Monroe, Iowa, and attended Central College in Pella, Iowa, and Ottawa University in Ottawa, Kansas. He lived in Wisconsin, Iowa, Nebraska, Missouri, and Kansas before moving to Little Rock, Arkansas. **Erwin McDonald,** standing, edits the *Arkansas Baptist Newsmagazine.*

A Look
Down the Lonesome
Road

A LOOK
DOWN THE LONESOME
ROAD

---

by Ralph Creger

with Erwin L. McDonald

Foreword by Harry Golden

DOUBLEDAY & COMPANY, INC.

GARDEN CITY, NEW YORK

1964

Library of Congress Catalog Card Number 64–14278
Copyright © 1964 by Ralph Creger
All Rights Reserved
Printed in the United States of America
First Edition

CONTENTS

FOREWORD

When the early Methodists of England waged their campaign
for the abolition of Negro slavery, the argument against them
was, "If only these outside agitators would leave us alone
everything would be all right."

In the American 1850s, the Southern slaveholders used the
same argument against the abolitionists, "If only the outside
agitators would leave us alone . . ."

During the current social revolution of the American
Negro, the important argument raised by the segregationists
is, "If only the outsiders would leave us alone . . ."

The social historian has every right to the observation that
racial segregation is really the psychological extension of slavery, since no new argument has been raised against it.

But this charge of "outside" interference is not only a fake
but a disservice to the South. The segregationists have in-
flicted greater damage on the South with this argument than
their attempt to ignore a federal court order. The segregationists have thus given the false impression that the South is a
monolithic society of racists, and in this process they dehu-
manize their own courageous people, the Ralph Cregers and
thousands of other white Southerners among whom are the
kindest people in the world.

This fake argument has obscured a fact that will be of great
value to the social historians of the future, namely that white
Southerners, Lillian Smith, Frank Graham, Guy Johnson,

Ralph McGill, Harry Ashmore (and I can name at least two hundred others) had more to do with encouraging the Negroes' drive for first-class citizenship than all the "outside" agitators combined.

I was on a speaking tour for the United States Eighth Army in the Far East. My lecture was on Abraham Lincoln and Carl Sandburg, but during the question-and-answer period I never heard the words, "Abraham Lincoln" or "Carl Sandburg." Every question was about "Little Rock," or "Faubus," or "What about the Negroes of the South?" I tried to tell the folks about the Ralph Cregers among the Southerners, and what their work has accomplished in attempting to resolve our moral crisis.

It is true that most of the white Southerners withdrew from this moral issue, but many stood and they stood in Little Rock, Arkansas, too, which is quite a story in itself, a story that Ralph Creger tells so well in this book.

Ralph Creger's efforts, his "letters to the editor," his articles, his word-of-mouth propaganda, and his pamphlet, *This Is What We Found*, not only gave Little Rock the better image it so richly deserved, but actually encouraged many other white Southerners to take the moral stand.

And it was not a simple decision for Ralph Creger to make. During the sixty-year life of "Jim Crow," those who had a vested interest in racial segregation had succeeded in making it an article of faith, of loyalty to the South. If you spoke out against it you were considered a renegade. This is one of the horrible myths that has helped perpetuate an evil system.

It is on this basis that Ralph Creger is correct in calling his book A LOOK DOWN THE LONESOME ROAD. It was indeed *lonesome* for a long time. While few men ever think of committing "treason," the Southerner has been conditioned to think of it every day of his life in connection with his Negro fellow-citizen.

I have followed the work of Ralph Creger during the years

since the United States Supreme Court Decision of May 17, 1954, which declared unconstitutional the segregation of the races in the public schools. I have found it interesting that Ralph Creger, like the Negros themselves, has been fighting this moral battle with Christianity as his weapon. The Negroes "in the streets" and thousands of Southern "Ralph Cregers" have rediscovered the Christian ethic, and it is they who are waging their fight against the dehumanizing concept of racism with the First Epistle of John: "He that saith, I know him, and keepeth not his commandments, is a liar, and the truth is not in him," and, "If a man say, I love God, and hateth his brother, he is a liar."

Harry Golden

A WORD
ABOUT THE SHARED AUTHORSHIP

Author Creger in his initial chapter and Harry Golden in the Foreword give a good orientation as to the approach, organization, and purpose of this book. Perhaps a few words are in order here on my part in the writing of the book, since I share in the by-line.

Far from being a co-author in the usual sense of the term, I have served, rather, as editor and friendly counselor. Really, I'm like a water boy who goes dashing out to "help" a baseball star who has just racked up a home run. For my friend Creger had worked on the manuscript for his book for many months and already had a tentative acceptance from the publishers before I came to have any official connection with the enterprise. At that juncture I accepted a joint invitation from the author and the publishers to assist in putting the manuscript into its final form. This has been a pleasant assignment, centering more on what, out of the Creger overflow, to leave out than what to put in.

Since this is largely the report of the personal experiences of the author and his family in searching for Christian attitudes and actions in coping with the race issue, I agreed from the beginning with the publishers that the story should be told in the first person and in the author's refreshing and frequently witty style.

While the author and I have similar views and attitudes on race, I do not necessarily agree with each and every expression found in his book. I have made no effort to "straighten him out" on any of his views, taking it, rather, as my task to help him any way I could to give the fullest and clearest expression to his ideas and viewpoints. My feeling is that we Americans have the best opportunity for working out an effective and harmonious solution to any problem, such as the race crisis, when we maintain and exercise our historic freedom to express our different views.

It is my sincere hope that the Creger book will be widely read and that it will help many to find the Christian solution to one of the greatest spiritual, moral, social, political, and economic problems of our time.

Erwin L. McDonald

Part One

LIFE AMONG THE GNAT-STRAINERS

Woe unto you, scribes and Pharisees, hypocrites! for ye pay tithe of mint and anise and cummin, and have omitted the weightier matters of the law, judgment, mercy, and faith: these ought ye to have done, and not to leave the other undone.

Ye blind guides, which strain at a gnat, and swallow a camel.

—Matthew 23:23–24

Chapter 1

HOW THIS BOOK
CAME TO BE WRITTEN

I have been a liberal on the race issue for as long as I have had any opinion at all about it. I'm not sure just how I got this way, but trying to determine the cause has been interesting.

In 1955 my family and I were transferred from Nebraska, where few people think about race, to Arkansas, where nearly everyone thinks about it.

On a warm September day in 1957 I had just come from a hospital visit during the noon hour and was preparing to drive back to my office. Just a few blocks away a mob was forming at Little Rock's Central High School. My better judgment told me to forget the excitement at the school and return to my office. But the whole business of trying to keep youngsters out of any public school just because of their color seemed so unreal to me that I just had to go and watch it.

As I parked my car and started walking toward the campus, a determined looking man got out of a car which bore an out-of-county license plate and fell into step beside me. Assuming, I suppose, that I felt as he did, he broke the silence, saying, "Well, I guess we'll soon have them 'black bastards' back where they belong!" I answered by saying that according to radio reports the Negro children had already been removed from the buildings, and so it was hard to see what the mob hoped to accomplish. "Oh," my companion continued, "we're going to *get* Blossom now!" (He was referring to School Superintendent Virgil Blossom.)

I had intended to maintain a discreet silence and should have, but blurted out, "Well, if that isn't about as stupid as you could get! Virgil Blossom is doing the best he can under the circumstances, and as far as I can see has come up with the most gradual plan you could reasonably expect."

At this point my erstwhile friend's countenance underwent an abrupt change and he spat out the question, "You a nigger lover?"

"Well," I replied, "I hadn't thought about it in just that way. Are you a 'nigger' hater?"

About this time we arrived at the outer fringe of a mass of humanity that seemed to extend for several blocks. Suddenly the man beside me pointed an accusing finger toward me and shouted, "He's a nigger lover—he thinks we're stupid!"

By this time I could see that I was the stupid one. Several men advanced toward me, but just at this time a huge roar went up a block away. Everyone turned and ran in the direction of the noise, not wanting to miss anything. Deciding that wisdom was much the better part of valor, I turned and walked back to my car. It was difficult for me to believe that what I had seen was occurring in the city of Little Rock, in the United States of America. I consoled myself with the thought that many of the demonstrators were from out of the city and out of the state and that the vast majority of Little Rock's citizens were *not* at the high school.

Later I had a good many sober second thoughts about my experience. What in the world, I asked myself, was an Iowa-born train dispatcher doing in the big middle of this sordid mess? Certainly I was not behaving in a typical manner. Many other railroad people in Little Rock also originated in Iowa or in other Midwestern states but seemed to be making a special effort to conform to local mores. Many tried to outdo the segregationists by being even more vehement in their denunciation of Eisenhower, the Supreme Court, and Negroes than were the out-and-out racists. I had the feeling that these transplants weren't fooling anyone, but, at least, they were keeping out of trouble.

So, why me? Why couldn't I have done like so many others and laughed at the racist when talking to fellow "imports" but agreed with him to his face?

Two turbulent years later, while our son Carl was enrolled in Central High, he and I collaborated in writing a book on prejudice. We were happy for this opportunity to speak out against bigotry and hate.

Probably any one who has been "published" suspects that he is a potential Hemingway. So I suppose it was only natural that I would have visions of writing a new and larger book which might easily become the twentieth-century *Uncle Tom's Cabin*, and a book which would surely cause racists to repent of their grievous sins against humanity. But it has gradually been made clear to me that books counseling against prejudice make few converts, as segregationists are not likely to spend their money for books telling them segregation is wrong. However, the realization that efforts to convert through writing are generally futile has not lessened my zeal. Once one gets involved in these social problems, there seems to be no turning back. And once one sees his thoughts in print, he never stops trying to get them there again. He finds himself "hooked" on both counts.

There is obviously little use in using conventional methods, or conventional arguments. So I have elected to write only to those who already agree with me. Quite frankly, this is a liberal's "handbook," designed to help the non-expert to be effective in trying to "Win Moderates" (to more positive action) and to "Influence Segregationists" (to become moderates). The first part of the book explains what motivated me, the second part attempts to motivate others, and the last part explains what we can do after being motivated.

Since I have been absolutely honest about my intentions, it would seem only fair for any racist who may have accidentally gotten this far in my book, to set it aside. I can see that it might be a temptation to continue, hoping to stumble upon the "do-gooder's" secrets. But we liberals don't go about reading *Common Sense*, White Citizens Council literature, Klan literature or the National States Rights Party's *Thunderbolt*. And so I say to you, Governor Wallace, *lay it down!* (We reserve the right to refuse service to anyone.)

I assume that my reading audience now consists only of those who think racial prejudice is wrong and would like to do something about it.

Many people know racial prejudice and discrimination are wrong but hesitate making their positions known. When an article I wrote, which urged Christian people to act like Christians in their race relations, appeared in Arkansas newspapers and a church news magazine, quite a few people in my church made it a point to let me know they liked what I had written, and that they wished more people would speak out on the matter. But most of them were careful to wait until they found me alone to pass out the bouquets. None sought me out when I was in a crowd to congratulate me. Finally, I complained wryly to a friend, "Look, I'm not trying to peddle some black-market product—just Christian ethics!"

Having to be careful about advocating compliance with Christ's teachings when one is in church defies all rules of reason and morality. It makes you wonder just what the shouting and the singing are all about. It is thoughts like these, I suppose, which create cynics, agnostics, or atheists. But faith is not easily discarded, and I wondered if my problem might not be that I had "seen the picture without having read the book."

I REREAD THE BIBLE

So I reread the Bible, with particular emphasis on the New Testament, since quite often people calling themselves "New Testament Christians" seem most inclined toward bigotry and prejudice. Rereading the scriptures restored my perspective. I discovered that there are no inconsistencies in Christ's teachings—just inconsistencies in men's application of them. Many preachers seem proud of their great fortitude, denouncing what they describe as worldly pleasures, but all the while displaying a callous indifference to the flagrant violations of many of Christ's important commandments.

One cannot help but wonder, after seeing these people twist and pervert the Bible's teachings just to pacify racists, if they would not do the same thing for other reasons if the price were right.

In fairness to the clergymen, we probably should not make a blanket indictment. There have always been those ministers, even in areas where racial segregation was rigidly enforced, who knew it was wrong and said so. This was true of a very small minority in Little Rock in 1957 and 1958. By 1963 the denunciation of racism had become more popular, and many church leaders did, at long last, begin to come to grips with the problem. One prominent churchman said, "We either accept the leadership that is ours, or we forfeit the right to be trusted."

Anyone who has been around churches and preachers very much knows that there are many times when ministers seem to consider it wise to "look the other way." Although we just naturally expect clergymen to be opposed to sin, we understand when preachers in Milwaukee or Peoria don't have quite so much to say about liquor as they do in Topeka or Nashville. We are aware pastors in Hollywood are less likely to denounce divorce than they would be if their pastorates were in Fort Smith or Bloomington. Men of the cloth in Las Vegas may not be quite as quick to denounce gambling as they would be in some other cities. We can understand these things. A certain amount of adjustment is expected according to local conditions. But in no area, save that of race relations, has a large portion of the church actually collaborated with those who make a mockery of Christ's teachings about love. And don't spoil this by recalling instances of paternalism, or of kindness at the personal level, but be honest and consider the kind of love that would cause you *really* to treat others as you would like to be treated. Tragic though it is, there are a good many preachers who go so far as actually to glorify a system in which people are often *afraid* to practice the Golden Rule. They defend their actions by talking about "tradition" and "our way of life."

Communists have said that religion is nothing but an opiate for the people. Many of us who do not believe this are grieved when preachers and church leaders say and do things because of race prejudice that would cause any thinking person to wonder.

I hesitated to say some of the things I have said for fear it would give skeptics and agnostics ammunition. But they are aware of all these inconsistencies, anyway, and it is my hope that they will search the scriptures to find the answers they seek. A colored minister who read the chapter "Humor in the Pulpit," told me he had thought he knew pretty well what white people were thinking and saying; but, he added, sadly, "I hadn't realized white preachers used 'Negro jokes' to 'warm up' their congregations." I suggested that exposing these things might do more harm than good. He assured me it would be best to "get it out in the open."

What I have written seems to be a strange admixture of optimism and pessimism, religious exhortations and cynicism, funny stories and lofty thoughts. But that's life, isn't it?

WEEPING WON'T HELP

At the National Conference of Religion and Race, held in Chicago, January 14–17, 1963, one of the speakers, speaking for white Protestants, said in effect: "It may be too late now for the church to act effectively. About all there is left to do is go home and weep!"[1] This may be overly pessimistic. I hope it is. If it is not, perhaps much of this book will be in vain. But I know how the speaker felt and why he said what he said. I know, because I have felt like weeping, too, at times.

I feel like weeping when I hear fine, wholesome, church-orientated young people getting their "kicks" from telling, or listening to, crude racial jokes.

I felt like weeping when I heard young people laugh and joke about the insults and indignities heaped upon Negro classmates during the troubled days of 1957, as I realized they were saying and doing these things because of what they had heard in their homes.

I felt like weeping when I remembered that not once did I hear any sort of advice or counsel to these young people from the pulpits of our churches.

I felt like weeping when I picked up a copy of *Life* magazine and saw the grief in the face of a small Negro boy whose father had been slain from ambush.

I have felt like weeping when I have had to listen to people vilify and insult the President of the United States and Supreme Court justices, simply because these people have been trying to make this country mean the same thing to Negro Americans that it does to others.

I have felt like weeping when hearing supposedly religious people, in this "land of opportunity," find it necessary,

[1] Chicago *Sun-Times*, January 15, 1963, page 3.

in order to bolster their own egos, to call their fellow Americans (always behind their backs, or at least in the safety of great numerical superiority) niggers, kikes, spiks, jigaboos, wops, fish eaters, dirty Jews, black bastards, krauts, coons, greaseballs, Polacks, etc., ad infinitum.

But weeping is not the answer, regardless of our inclinations. The Negroes, who have had real cause to weep, have done little of it. Many have laughed when there was little to laugh at. They have laughed in order to survive. But they are not laughing so much these days. At least they have quit laughing at things that are not funny.

Author Richard Wright, in his autobiography *Black Boy* (page 159), tells of his reaction to the treatment of Negro patrons in a Mississippi store where he was employed as a janitor. He wrote, "Each day in the store I watched the brutality with growing hate, yet trying to keep my feelings from registering in my face. When the boss looked at me I would avoid his eyes. Finally the boss's son cornered me one morning.

" 'Say, nigger, look here,' he began.

" 'Yes, sir.'

" 'What's on your mind?'

" 'Nothing sir,' I said, trying to look amazed, trying to fool him.

" 'Why don't you laugh and talk like the other niggers?' he asked.

" 'Well, sir, there's nothing much to say or smile about,' I said, smiling.

"His face was hard, baffled; I knew that I had not convinced him. He whirled from me and went to the front of the store; he came back a moment later, his face red. He tossed a few green bills at me.

" 'I don't like your looks, nigger. Now, get!' he snapped."

So the other Negroes, who were not so brilliant but who may have had more prudence, stayed on and continued to laugh. But Wright left Mississippi and eventually left America.

The racist has not been too difficult to get along with, either for the white liberal or for the Negro, as long as we haven't gotten too serious. And since it may be a good idea to "fight fire with fire," this book is not one to cause weeping, but rather laughter.

The laughter is just pointed in an unusual direction.

I once heard the story of a college professor lecturing his class about the rare and strange "woofle bird," whose unusual characteristic is that it lays eggs three times its own size. "These," the professor solemnly told his class, "are not happy birds."

The people we are concerned about are not "happy people." They are not happy because they have gone through travail similar to that of the woofle bird. They try to appear happy, as they tell their jokes about the "ole nigger preacher" and about "Kennedy's Koon Klan," but their laughter is beginning to sound increasingly hollow—sometimes embarrassed and often frightened. They are not happy because they claim to be a religious people but have become addicted to straining at various doctrinal gnats and swallowing camels three times their own size—the camel of man's inhumanity to man in the form of racial prejudice. Such maneuvers, of course, defy all laws of nature and science, and the strain is beginning to tell.

These are those who will question my qualifications to write a book about racial prejudice. It would be nice if I could say that I grew up in the South and started out with all of the standard concepts of race, then suddenly saw the blinding light, as Paul did on the road to Damascus. But it wasn't this way.

However, I may have more qualifications than those immediately apparent. Many of my friends who have been active in various human-rights endeavors did grow up in the

South. They have given me much insight into various aspects
of the race problem. These are the people who have really
suffered, and they deserve much credit. After nine years in a
city wracked part of the time by race problems which were
real and the rest of the time by the false hopes and false
fears encouraged by politicians, it has become clear to me that
objectivity is difficult for those who have been encouraged in
their prejudices from earliest childhood and are accustomed
to life in a society which has demanded conformity.

During the past fifteen years I have read hundreds of books
on social problems. Most of my segregationist friends have
read none of these books.

For the past fifteen years I have talked to and become acquainted with many colored people, trying to determine how
they feel and why they feel as they do. My segregationist
friends tell me they never discuss human rights with Negroes.

Many of the Negroes I know are leaders in the community.
They are ministers, teachers, doctors, and lawyers. None of
my segregationist friends know any of these people.

In 1961 I appeared on a television panel show in New York
with author James Baldwin. This was very enlightening. I felt
that Mr. Baldwin was a little bit rough on white liberals, and
that he might not be fully aware of our problems. But then,
we certainly are not fully aware of his.

My family and I have listened to lectures by outstanding
Negro leaders such as Dr. Samuel Sheppard. Dr. Sheppard is
a St. Louis educator who has received national recognition for
his work in raising achievement levels of children from culturally handicapped backgrounds to levels at or above the national average. We have discussed civil rights with such men
as Carl Rowan, now Director of the United States Information Agency.

Because of my writing, many well-known Americans have
written me. Much of this correspondence has been helpful.
It seemed to provide clues as to why we, as a nation, often

fall far short of practicing what we preach for many of those who wrote seemed to be masters of double talk. There were some notable exceptions, of course.

I have known, personally, many of the colored children who have attended Little Rock's integrated schools. Among them are straight-A and other honor students, from junior and senior high schools.

I have participated in athletic contests, with and against, colored players. Few of my segregationist friends have done this.

Yet racists would say I do not understand. They talk about interracial sex. This is one area in which the racist may have had more experience than I, for I have had none.

It has dawned on me that since I have worked so hard trying to find the answers, I might have more insight into the problems of race relations than my detractors have.

I have listened carefully to what people said about Negroes, Jews, Mexicans, Catholics, and about any group that has been the object of prejudice at one time or another. I believe that the people who did the talking were more likely to reveal their true feelings to a railroad dispatcher than they would to a known "expert"—since the expert just might write a book about it all!

Chapter 2

THAT'S WHERE
THE TALL CORN GROWS

We're from I-oway, I-oway
State of all the land,
Joy on every hand . . .
That's where the tall corn grows!

This is the song we all sang lustily around the bandstand in the city park each Thursday night in the summertime, at the Monroe, Iowa, weekly band concert. In Iowa, the main interest is corn and hogs and ever-normal granaries. Iowans are still mad because the locale of the movie *State Fair* was transferred from Iowa, where it really happened, to Texas. In addition to farming, Iowans manufacture various items such as tractors, plows, combines, and even washing machines.

About the only race I ever heard anything about when I was a boy was the annual auto race at the state fair in Des Moines. So the small Midwestern farming community where I grew up would hardly seem a likely spawning ground for an ardent civil-rights crusader.

However, psychologists say that most of our actions are the indirect result of some previous experience, and in order to understand why a person behaves as he does it is necessary to discover that person's earlier experiences—particularly the emotionally upsetting ones.

Scientists say that for every action there is an equal and opposite reaction.

Sociologists tell us that they see human life as the product of social interaction between persons and groups.

Ecologists insist that we are the product of our environment, which they describe as the sum of all external forces acting on an organism or community of organisms.

The Bible says, "Train up a child in the way he should go; and when he is old he will not depart from it" (Proverbs 22:6).

If all these things are true, then somewhere in my Iowa background lies the answer as to why I now think as I do.

I can understand that the average reader would not be greatly interested in what caused my liberal tendencies. Some might want to find out why President Johnson, or Senator Eastland of Mississippi, or Governor Rockefeller of New York, or Governor Wallace of Alabama feel as they do about prejudice and related matters. But if I can discover why I became so liberal on the race issue, then maybe by the same process I can see what makes the racist tick. What I really would like to accomplish is to inspire the reader to examine his own background to find out how prejudiced he is and how he got that way. This is important because prejudice is a good deal like alcoholism; the most difficult part is admitting that you have a problem. At least this has been my experience.

My research into my past has provided me with many of the answers I sought. I believe I now understand what caused a fundamentalist Baptist, Midwestern, conservative, Hoover Republican to wind up as an orthodox Southern Baptist, liberal, New Frontier Democrat.

As is the case with most young men in small towns, the things that seemed most important to me were sports, sex, money, and religion. In order to judge their relevance and their effects on future attitudes, it will be necessary to explore each of these areas briefly.

In Monroe, as in many small Midwestern towns, about the only outlet for young men wishing to demonstrate their physical prowess was high school basketball. In the twenties we were particularly proud because "our boys" were seemingly unbeatable and even managed to beat Newton, the county seat, in the tournament. Tournament time was the season of the year we all waited patiently for, but one of the contests which made a lasting impression was just a regular conference game. We were playing Colfax, a nearby town, and the reason for the unusual amount of interest was that Colfax had a Negro player—an unusual situation in those days. So we all lined up early the night of the Colfax game in order to get a good seat for this encounter that had the whole town talking.

I must confess that there seemed to be considerable disappointment in evidence as the visiting team came dashing out. The Negro boy seemed to have pretty much the same size, movements, and talent that the rest of the team displayed. We felt let down.

"He must be a lot better than the other boys," I heard one spectator remark, "else they wouldn't let him play!"

After the game started, interest continued to center on the dark-skinned competitor. When the Colfax team fell behind, one fellow remarked, "Typical! typical! Put the pressure on *them* and they fold up." But when the colored boy intercepted a pass and put his team back in the lead, another expert commented: "You got to admit *they* are good athletes." Once during the game, a stray dog found its way into the gymnasium and wandered out on the playing floor. The referee had to stop the contest while he ejected the offender. Nearly everyone, including the Negro athlete, was convulsed with laughter.

An elderly gentleman remarked: "*They* sure got a sense of humor!"

It was obvious to me, even at nine years of age, that everything the Negro boy did had a special significance. About the only one there who did not make a big production out of his presence was the colored player. He just kept "popping them in."

Later, when I played on the team, we had high hopes of "going all the way" to the state tournament. Somehow we never managed it. But we always got there as spectators, for the entire five-day period. For us it was *the* big holiday. Our real interest, I think, was in the possibility that there might be an upset. Iowa had a tournament in which schools of all sizes competed, without regard to class. Consequently, there were occasions when small villages, generally unknown before their tournament successes, "knocked off" one of the giants, such as Waterloo, Des Moines, or Sioux City. I think we subconsciously felt that the boys from the small towns out there under the floodlights were really representing our town, in these David vs. Goliath confrontations.

WE WERE SURE WE WEREN'T BIGOTS

I can recall one of these games particularly well. Sioux City (population 80,000) was playing Winfield (population 800). Naturally, the crowd's sympathies lay with Winfield. During the heat of battle, a colored boy playing for Sioux City inadvertently crashed into one of Winfield's most popular players—a little redhead who had captured the fancy of the fans in previous games. Immediately, a sustained and ominous BOOOOoooooo arose from the more than fifteen thousand fans. But a minute later, when the half ended, the two boys simultaneously strode toward each other, shook hands, and then walked off the floor together talking and laughing. The huge throng rose as one man in a standing ovation. Here was proof, we thought, that Iowans were not bigots. We wanted no part of racial prejudice. Of course, if a Negro had moved next door to most of the people doing the cheering, they'd have been in a state of panic. But this was different, we told ourselves. We remained standing and continued to cheer.

Certain physical and psychological changes generally occur in boys at the age of twelve or thirteen. Voices fluctuate wildly, "peach fuzz" appears on the cheeks, and other signs of manhood become evident and are a source of great pride to those fortunate enough to be a little precocious. But it seemed to me that fate had been most unkind. At the age of fourteen, when most of my friends were dashing proudly and unadorned from locker to shower room with a "nothing to hide" air, I was having to make furtive dashes after making sure that no one was looking. But time heals all things, and at sixteen I realized that things were, at long last, different. Or better still, they were, at long last, the same. So at this time I felt an obligation, insofar as my relationship to the opposite sex was concerned. I certainly didn't have a great deal going for me, as I had a face that only a mother could love, due to an acute case of acne that had caused my sister to remark, helpfully, "Well, at least there isn't room for many more pimples."

Under such circumstances it would probably have been wise for me to select a young lady also lacking in physical charm, as the object of my affection. But because of what I considered a sparkling personality and a never-say-die attitude, I pursued relentlessly one of the most attractive girls in school for about two years. It finally dawned on me that there had been virtually no reciprocity. So I asked her quite bluntly just why it was that she wouldn't go out with me.

"Well," she retorted, "since you ask me, I just plain don't like you."

Now you just can't get it put to you much more frankly than that, and I finally got the point. But I had the feeling that I had been the victim of a gigantic conspiracy of some sort. This may have been one of the things that soured me on discrimination, as I certainly felt I was being discriminated against. But in this area it may be that I am grasping at straws.

There seems, generally, to be a connection between economics and civil rights. People liberal in one field are usually liberal in the other. I suspect that if prolonged unemployment for myself and others had not made me a political liberal early in life, I might not have been nearly so sympathetic toward the Negroes and their efforts to obtain the same basic citizenship rights the rest of us consider our birthright.

It should surprise no one that the self-styled rugged individualists who complain about government spending for the benefit of our people as a whole nearly always oppose any steps that our government suggests to help eliminate exploitation of minority groups in particular. These people will tell you that a little exploitation, like a little unemployment, might not be such a bad thing, and that if you happened to be the one getting exploited, why, this is just the way the ball bounces—survival of the fittest, and all of that.

So, if the people who believe strictly in letting nature take its economic course do not lie awake nights worrying about the exploitation of people in general, they will certainly lose little sleep because Negroes are taken advantage of now and then.

The gimmick of exploiting the Negro's vulnerable position on the labor market was no factor in the economic life of Monroe, Iowa, in the late twenties and early thirties. But I am convinced that the Great Depression and the subsequent change in our political thinking played a major role in shaping my future thoughts and actions about basic human rights for all Americans.

Nowadays we hear some "segregation-now-and-forever" politicians warning us to be on the lookout for communists. It may be that these gentlemen have seen some communists around, but the only people I ever knew who indicated they might be even casually interested in communism were folks who had been out of work a long time, some thirty years ago. And these people soon lost their interest after FDR got into high gear.

But back to Monroe and my early impressions. There are many things about small towns that leave their marks on impressionable boys. You can discount none of them, from the weekly concerts in the park to the yearly extravaganzas such as Old Settlers' Day. But perhaps in my case, the thing that made a really lasting impression was the preaching.

THE MOST TALENTED GNAT-STRAINERS

I have a great deal to say about people I refer to as gnat-strainers, and others I call camel-swallowers. I did not have a great deal of experience with the camel-swallowers until recent years. I have had long years of experience with highly skilled gnat-strainers. And I have learned, from moving about, that a really proficient gnat-strainer can nearly always manage to swallow a camel three times his own size. What I am saying is that there is a very close kinship between religious bigotry and racial bigotry. They are first cousins at the very least.

Some of the most talented of the gnat-strainers are preachers. I know, because they had me straining, too, for many years. Even today it is hard for me to criticize these men because, after all, they do preach against sin. And you just can't argue a great deal with that. But after thinking back about all the sermons I have heard, it suddenly dawned on me that seldom, if ever, did the gnat-straining preachers who were mighty finicky about some of the sins they were discussing do more than generalize about some of the sins Christ put particular emphasis on.

No doubt many of the things that happened in Monroe were typical of happenings in like-sized communities elsewhere. But there were differences. Unless prejudice is recognized for what it is, most people just naturally seem to enjoy having someone to feel superior to, or look down on; to dislike or mistrust. People in most larger cities are blessed with a large enough Jewish minority, or some other minority, to accommodate their basic needs. On the West Coast, Orientals frequently have supplied the necessary outlet, as have the Indians in South Dakota and the Mexicans in the Southwest. Negroes have been ideal where they have been present. But Monroe was 99 per cent Caucasian and Protestant. So it was difficult to assert superiority, although I am sure we'd have done a fine job, given the opportunity. There was Ikey, the junk dealer, but it would have been hard to convince the citizenry that he represented a threat to their economic security, or was about to "mongrelize the race." There was one Catholic family, but they didn't even have a church to attend; so it would have been hard to convince the people these Catholics were in on some sort of an international conspiracy.

You can see we had a real problem. The void was partially filled by an intense rivalry which developed between the three Protestant churches in the community. The local preachers in these churches were usually careful not to go too far in their accusations about the other churches, but sometimes, when guest speakers were brought in for revivals, the rules were suspended, and if they mentioned the possibility that one of the other churches might be a tool of the communists, this was just their ministerial privilege. And our visiting evangelists were usually very convincing orators.

One Sunday night, when I was fourteen, we had a missionary from Burma as guest speaker. His sermon dealt with the similarities between sin and leprosy. His portrayal was so vivid and his delivery so forceful that by the end of the sermon I not only realized I was a sinner, but I was also convinced I had leprosy. The more I thought about the matter the more I realized the horrible truth. One morning when getting dressed I noticed a small white spot between my toes, and this confirmed my already strong conviction. At school that day I went to the library and looked up the word "leprosy," and this eliminated any doubts I may have had as the definition stated, "The disease is usually preceeded by melancholia—a depressed mental state." There could be no further doubt about the matter, I thought. So I confided in my parents about my condition and insisted that I get immediate medical attention. They finally agreed to send me up to see "Doc Mac," our family physician, who soon sent me out the door with a whack on the seat of my breeches saying all the matter with me was that I had trichophytosis, which I later found meant athlete's foot. I have always felt he could have been a little more considerate, in view of my depressed mental state.

It was obvious that there wasn't much doubt in the minds of our evangelists that most other churches had "modernistic" leanings. They didn't preach the gospel, we were told. When they did it was the "social gospel," and this was even worse. It was rumored that some of the Sunday school teachers in the other churches played bridge, and we had it on good authority that one of them smoked cigarettes. So we voted to discontinue joining with these other churches in any more "union" services.

Sometimes I had secret doubts about the things that were going on. I wondered if, maybe, some of the ministers and church leaders might not be more concerned with being fundamentalists than they were with being Christians, and more zealous in trying to ferret out "modernists" than in trying to follow a lot of Christ's most important teachings, such as, "Judge not that ye be not judged . . . let him who is without sin among you first cast a stone . . . By this shall all men know that ye are my disciples, because ye love one another."

But I was smart enough to keep my thoughts to myself. Besides, I had gotten quite a reputation myself for being able to spot a modernist when I heard one. All of this certainly lent excitement and drama to what otherwise might have been rather dull Sunday evenings.

Nearly everyone in town went to church and I always attended with my good friend "Mouse," a youth of like ideas and interest. As to the matter of church attendance, I had no choice. Mouse could have avoided going, but he was my good friend, and, besides, I had the car. We really didn't mind going anyway, as there was always an ample supply of the town's young womanhood present. Mouse and I always intended to muster up the courage, after services, to charm a couple of "wimmen" into getting into our car with us. (In Monroe, at that period in history, girls thirteen to twenty-one were always called "wimmin" by young men in the same age bracket. When they became adults they were "girls" again.)

Usually, when church was dismissed, we just stood out on the front steps sheepishly, and watched the equally embarrassed "wimmen" walk right on by. But then we'd get in the car and tear around the town square, looking them over carefully, honking, and talking about the "wimmen" we'd get next Sunday.

In the meantime we heard lots of sermons and absorbed at least a part of what we heard. As for myself, I must admit to being troubled by much of it. I recall one night in particular, as Mouse and I squirmed on the hard pews, listening intently to the words pouring out at us. "Yes, my brethren," the evangelist was shouting, "they will tell you that I scare people, and this is true. If I could scare you out of hell, I'd gladly do it."

"I'll bet he could switch those words around and still be telling the truth," I whispered to Mouse. But immediately I felt guilty for what I had said.

A few minutes later, as sometimes happened, I dozed off. Suddenly I saw all sorts of brightly lit words, flashing off and on as though they were signboards such as you'd see on

Broadway. They kept flashing brighter and brighter, and they read: MODERNIST, HIGHER CRITICISM, HARRY EMERSON FOS-DICK, LAKE OF FIRE, DANCING, APOSTASY, CIGARETTES, FLASK, FOUR HORSEMEN, DAYS OF NOAH, SOCIAL GOSPEL, JEAN HARLOW, BRIDGE CLUBS, VILE SINNERS, LIPSTICK, MASONRY, ROUGE, GOLF ON SUNDAY, SUNDAY PAPERS.

Suddenly, the evangelist emitted a piercing shriek that precluded any further slumber. I awoke with a start. "Yes, my brethren," he was saying, "often, in these last days those doing the greatest damage to the Lord's work are found right in our pulpits!"

I felt as though my head would split. Why did they insist on making everything so complicated? I wondered. It was supposed to be so simple—only believe and have faith. But they wouldn't leave it that way. They insisted on adding a million more rules!

There was a Bible in the rack in front of me and I started to leaf through it. I came across the 22d chapter of Matthew, and read, beginning with verse 35: "Then one of them, which was a lawyer, asked him a question, tempting him and saying, Master, which is the greatest commandment in the law? Jesus said unto him, *Thou shalt love the Lord thy God with all thy heart, and with all thy soul, and with all thy mind. This is the first and great commandment. And the second is like unto it, Thou shalt love thy neighbor as thyself.* On these two commandments hang all the law and the prophets."

Suddenly I relaxed. I had wanted a simple explanation, and I had found it, and from the real authority! I knew I could not explain away the complicated universe and its operation without admitting to the presence of God. No one should try to dodge these issues, I thought. It seemed to me God had put man on the world and given him certain rules of conduct. He had told man how he could have eternal life, and how he could have a satisfying life here on earth. But man wasn't satisfied, and insisted on adding a few thousand rules of his own. He couldn't seem to handle these. So God gave Moses the Ten Commandments. This satisfied the people for a while, but before long they got to improvising their own rules again. So God sent His Son to save men from their sins and also to straighten them out a little. And this time He cut the number of rules down to two.

About this time the preacher closed his sermon with a remark about seeing church members around a bridge table, as he drove home from church the preceding Sunday.

But I relaxed and waited for the closing hymn. Maybe, I mused, some of the other folks could get their "real peace" from the flow of words coming at them from the pulpit. Most of them were older and probably could remember a lot more. But Christ had cut the number of rules down to two, and I believed I could handle them.

So I nudged Mouse and muttered: "Let's get out fast, and get the car parked by the front steps before the 'wimmen' come out."

Chapter 3

RACIAL PREJUDICE—
NORTHERN STYLE

During my formative years I had only the vaguest notion as
to what prejudice was. People in Iowa just don't think about
things like that. Mostly, they wonder if there will be so much
rain it will hurt the corn, or if there will be so little rain it
will hurt the corn. Sometimes they wonder if their town's
basketball team has a chance to make it to the state tournament, and sometimes they get pretty excited about the University's football team. But about the only minority group
they ever worry about is the farmer, and they have done a
pretty good job of looking out for this particular oppressed
minority. Nevertheless, my first brush with race prejudice occurred not in Arkansas, not in Alabama, not in Mississippi,
but in Iowa, where Negro quarterbacks lead their teams to
conference championships, and where the law, editorial opinion, and the clergy all stand firm against denial of rights to
people because of race.

In 1946, we bought a home in Des Moines where I was
night dispatcher for the railroad. It was not in the part of
town we would have preferred, but it was the best we could
afford and it was close to my work. A few days after we moved
in a stranger stopped to see us, and asked us if we knew we
had Negro neighbors. The way he put the question to us it
sounded a good deal as though he was asking us if we were

aware there was leprosy in the community. I said that we did not know our neighbors' race and were not worried a great deal about it. Our benefactor then explained that he knew we were from a small town and needed help on such matters. He said that he personally had nothing against Negroes, and was entirely sympathetic with their aims, and that he even contributed to the N.A.A.C.P. But, he continued, we had to face facts! "Like it or not, they do depress property values." The people across the street were fine folks, he agreed, but they owned the entire block, and it was rumored that they planned to sell two of the houses to Negroes. We could easily imagine, he confided, what this would do to the value of our property. He went on to say that he would be glad to find us another home, and that it would be well to check thoroughly on the neighborhood. He knew of a nice home on the West Side that he could get for us "for a song." It was well, he said, to be sure about Jews in the neighborhood too. He hated to say this, he admitted, because some of his best friends were Jews.

It was obvious to us that we had to act quickly. So we listed our house with this salesman who had been so considerate. We were not acting because of prejudice, we told ourselves, we just had to protect our investment. Time went by and no one seemed interested in buying. Finally, the agent asked if we would consider selling "to colored." We told him it certainly didn't matter to us, just as long as we did not lose our investment. The next night a congenial Negro agent stopped by and asked about showing the home to prospective buyers. We visited awhile, then, suddenly, he looked me squarely in the eye and asked, "Does the fact that my people live across the street have anything to do with your decision to sell?"

"No," I lied, "it's just that I sleep days, and there is so much traffic on this street that I can't rest."

This was not one of my prouder moments. I was lying; he

knew I was lying, and he knew I knew I wasn't fooling him at all.

Eventually the house was sold, to white people. The neighbor across the street did not sell any of his houses. And soon after that the state bought the entire block for office buildings and everyone made a nice profit—but me.

This incident was, I think, the thing that really started me thinking, reading about, and observing the phenomenon of race prejudice. And to any of my readers who happen to be colored, here is something to think about: If the real estate agent, the second one, had behaved in Uncle Tom fashion, been a yes-man, and catered to my prejudices, all the things I had heard about Negroes would have been confirmed in my mind. But he didn't come "hat in hand." And he didn't mind losing a sale, if necessary, for a principle. I was impressed.

MY FRIEND THE REDCAP

From then on I read every book on race and social problems I could get my hands on. I talked with people about it. I got pretty well acquainted with some of the colored railroad employees. One of them, a redcap, was quite a sports fan. So we talked a lot about basketball and about players we had both known years before. I didn't realize that my friend was dissatisfied with his lot, since he made about $300 a month as a redcap and another $300 "moonlighting" on another job when not on duty at the railroad station. But one day he told me bitterly that there was a job opening for a ticket clerk, and that he had asked for it but was told he could not work the job, even if there were no other applicants. He asked me why this should be, since he was a high school graduate, had done well in school, and was much more familiar with railroad operations than most people. I agreed with him that it was unfair but shrugged it off as something I could do nothing about.

In 1953 we were transferred to Fairbury, Nebraska, where I was chief dispatcher for the road's western division which stretched from Des Moines to Colorado Springs. There were few Negroes in Fairbury, but those who were there were pretty well integrated. One family attended the same church we did. No one worried about Negroes, as there were other minority groups to occupy their attention. Quite a few Mexicans worked for the railroad, but none held jobs that could be classed as skilled. They had been denied employment as trainmen or enginemen. The men already working said emphatically they would refuse to work with them.

In northeastern Nebraska and in South Dakota there were a good many Indians. Traveling around over the territory, we noticed that nearly all Indians seemed to live in crudely built homes, drove ancient pickup trucks, and seemed to be entirely devoid of ambition or incentive. I inquired about this and was told it was only through the benevolence of the white man that these Sioux Indians managed as well as they did. One friend who owned land near a reservation complained because most of the Indians seemed to prefer to stay on their reservation and draw government checks rather than get out and find employment or go to college.

"Why don't they get a job, like Negroes do?" my friend asked. The usual explanation I got was that Indians were just not equipped to compete in the complex American life of today. Nearly everyone insisted, though, that they personally had never been unkind or mistreated an Indian. Through it all I could not help remembering a man generally conceded to be one of the great military geniuses of all time, Chief Crazy Horse, a Lakota Sioux!

One of my duties at Fairbury was to interview prospective employees. Each spring we normally hired a new group of

apprentice telegraphers. Most of these men came from a telegraph school in Pueblo, Colorado. My first group looked
much like the ordinary crew-cut set—average American boys
of eighteen or nineteen—except that one of them was a very
dark-skinned Mexican. I could see that his arrival did not
meet with the approval of most of the employees in the
building. One of them, knowing I was new to the region,
came to me and told me Mexicans were just not hired for
work as telegraph operators, or for anything else much, on the
railroad, except to work "on the section." He said it was common knowledge that the Mexicans were not usually intelligent
enough to handle skilled work, and that, in addition, they
were lazy and untrustworthy. I thanked my informer but in-
terviewed the dark-skinned boy as well as the rest. The young
man did well on his IQ test and on the other phases of the
patterned interview. But, of course, the printed forms said
nothing about race. When we had finished I asked if he
realized the difficulties he might encounter because of his race.
He said he certainly did and seemed relieved that I had
brought the matter up. He told me about sacrifices he and
his parents had made so that he could prepare himself for a
good job. He then became quite emotional and said something about having studied in school that America was a
country where anyone could get ahead, if he worked hard
enough. He said he often wondered if it wasn't all "a big lie."
When he had calmed down I told him he was going to get the
job. I asked him not to let me down. He never did! I shall
never forget the look on that Mexican boy's face when he
learned he was actually going to get a decent, skilled job.

In 1954 we read with interest news items about the Supreme Court's public school desegregation decision. Some of
my railroad friends originated in the South and gave me several reasons why integration in the South would simply not
work. They told me there was a different class Negro in the

South. I realized that these people spoke from experience. But I wished I could somehow watch the unfolding drama from a closer vantage point. I had no idea that I ever would.

Then in 1955 we were transferred to Little Rock, Arkansas!

Part Two

TRYING TO SWALLOW
A CAMEL

. . . and swallow a camel . . .
(Matthew 23:24)

Chapter 4

AN IOWA YANKEE
IN KING ORVAL'S COURT

By now, a good many millions of words have been written about Little Rock. Journalists, preachers, lawyers, sociologists, educators, and assorted advocates have had important things to say about the unhappy events that began at Central High and registered their impact across the face of the globe. Great issues of law and of political and social change had their focus at Little Rock. So it was only natural that many experts felt led to make literary contributions, explaining what had happened and why. But for an Iowa-born railroad dispatcher and his teen-age son to try and to be successful in joining this select group was considered by some as merely a lucky break and by others as an unfortunate accident.

However, as previously indicated, my son and I did write a book about Little Rock. We tried to write as southerners. We consider ourselves southerners, even though we did originate in Iowa—southern Iowa, that is. Of course, we are aware that a lot of people have the idea that the South and racial prejudice go hand in hand. We have found that this just "ain't necessarily so!"

We became southerners because of longer and fewer railroad trains, which in turn resulted in fewer railroad dispatching offices. But whatever the reason, we hadn't lived in Little Rock long until we felt we were home.

My family in 1955 consisted of my wife Barbara, who grew up in Newton, Iowa, and our son Carl, who had been born in Iowa and had lived with us in Iowa, Missouri, Kansas, Illinois, and Nebraska.[1]

All we knew of Arkansas was, as Will Rogers might have put it, "what we read in the papers." We expected to find life and the people in Arkansas very different from life and the people we had known. I can state emphatically after nine years in Little Rock that reports of such differences are much like the erroneous report of Mark Twain's death—"highly exaggerated."

It was the similarities, not the differences, which surprised us. Little Rock is surprisingly like Des Moines. The cities are about the same size and both are capitals of agricultural states. Neither has a great deal of industry—both are working on this. Historically they have been the shopping and cultural centers of two very similar states.

When we moved to Little Rock we immediately felt more at home than we had in various eastern cities we had visited. The slight differences in speech were of no major consequence and seemed less strange to me than accents I had heard in Chicago and New York.

I have become particularly sympathetic to what I have discovered is the Arkansan's pet peeve, unflattering remarks about the state by outsiders. It is all too easy to recall a similar resentment we had in Iowa, when visitors showed up from some eastern metropolis and called us sod-busters, or hayseeds.

Now it doesn't matter a great deal whether they call you a hayseed or a hillbilly. The degree of resentment is about the same. You do not appreciate it. Usually, you know that you would not exchange places with the visitors for all their ap-

[1] We adopted a second son, Jerry, in 1959, when he was eight years old.

parent sophistication. The Iowa farmer often managed to overlook his classification in the solace of Liberace, "crying all the way to the bank." Arkansans may not have had this solution quite so frequently, but may have soon, for few states have more natural resources and potential for industrial and economic growth than does Arkansas.

But the most important resources of a city, state, or nation are its churches, its schools, and its people. We are convinced that the churches, the schools, and the people we have become a part of in Little Rock are second to none.

In 1957, Carl was critically injured in a motor scooter accident and was rushed to a hospital. We had to wait for several hours before we were told that he was going to be all right. As we returned to the hospital waiting room, we found more than twenty of our church friends waiting for us, wanting to know if there was something they could do to help. This and other gestures of friendship and good will are the rule in Little Rock, not the exception. Later, in 1957, we wished there were some way we could let all the world know about the love and compassion that motivates so many of the people in Little Rock. Since 1960 we have been privileged to tell many.

"GOOD GUYS" AND "BAD GUYS"

As to pretended differences between such states as Iowa and Arkansas, Indiana and Tennessee, Pennsylvania and Georgia, we have found that Americans everywhere are pretty much alike, and that you'll find the "good guys" and the "bad guys" wherever you go, even though they may be referred to in one area as "youse guys" and in other places as "good old boys." We have discovered that if you want to have friends, you have to be a friend, and that this principle applies regardless of geography.

Of course, just about everyone knows what the difference

is supposed to be. It's integration, segregation, race relations
—call it what you will, it is ever present in many of these
United States. In these states race seems to lurk in the back
of nearly everyone's mind, and, sooner or later enters every
conversation, and calculation, with words spoken or unspoken.
It is the only thing of importance that is present in Arkansas
but absent in Iowa. It is the only difference that matters. And
this difference has nothing to do with innate prejudice in the
people of either region, but is the result only of an accident of
history and geography.

Some of the prejudice we witnessed in the upper Midwest
was as cruel and intense as any we have seen in Arkansas. To
make matters worse, the people in Iowa have never been able
to try and justify their prejudice by talking of custom, fear,
or the desire to conform. Obviously, it is easier for the Iowa
or Minnesota farmer to claim freedom from prejudice than it
is for the farmer in Arkansas, Mississippi, or Alabama. There
are few Negroes around for the northern farmers to be prejudiced against. Politicians in the North have found it unprofit-
able to beat on the black bogey man. So the farmers in Iowa
and Minnesota are able to drive to Iowa City, or Minneapolis,
on crisp fall days, and watch Negro quarterbacks, halfbacks,
and fullbacks lead their teams to victory. Then they can all
silently commend themselves for their tolerance in letting
these Negro athletes come and help them win championships.

Although there is hypocrisy in such states as Iowa and Minnesota you find many examples of good race relations and
equal justice there, too. I get a little weary of hearing
about how *all* of the people in the North are hypocritical in
their attitudes on race, because I know it isn't so. There are
people, and there are cities, in the North, that make a real effort to help the Negro obtain his fair share of the blessings
of American citizenship, just as there are in the South. I
think it time we gave credit where credit is due, by talking
about what goes on locally, in cities and towns, rather than

trying to praise, or else condemn, an entire state or region. Atlanta, Georgia, does well, while other Georgia cities are slower to discard the chains that bind them. And I am sure we can find parallels in North Carolina, Illinois, Tennessee, and all other states.

The Des Moines, Iowa, schools were never segregated. Some of their schools have no Negroes because of discrimination in housing; some have only a few colored students; and a few have a Negro majority. North High must have two or three hundred colored students. There are colored students in all of Des Moines' six high schools. Percentage estimates are difficult to get, as teachers say they think of the children only as students. A former neighbor, who teaches in North High, seemed amused when I asked him questions about disease, discipline problems, and low educational standards because of Negroes. He said he certainly couldn't see much of a health problem, judging by the number of Negro athletes on their teams, and that the Des Moines schools were rated among the best in the nation, scholastically. And he said he had the statistics to prove it. He did agree that conditions might easily be different in large cities, such as New York, Washington, or Chicago, but that such cities had delinquency problems before they had many Negroes, when other racial and nationality groups made up the troubled minority. As to racially mixed marriages, my friend told me that if there ever had been one in Des Moines schools, he had not heard of it. He said that Negroes participated fully in all extracurricular activities; that, as far as he had been able to observe, selections for athletic teams, bands, and honor societies had been based entirely on merit and ability.

I certainly am not trying to imply that just because public schools in Des Moines, Iowa, are and always have been integrated, that schools in Little Rock, Arkansas, should, necessarily, be desegregated. But I do think that having lived in both regions and observing both systems in operation helps me separate fact from fiction. Experiences in Des Moines and in other Midwestern cities taught me many things.

I knew that the Des Moines schools were nationally recognized for their excellence and were a part of a state school system which had produced the nation's highest rate of literacy (over 99 per cent).

Seeing and attending these Midwestern integrated schools and colleges convinced me that the pictures painted by the White Citizens Councils and other groups were sheer figments of the imagination and products of wishful thinking. I didn't doubt that examples of trouble could be found in such places as New York, Chicago, or Washington, D.C. But I also felt that in such large cities it would indeed have been remarkable if instances of racial or class trouble never occurred. However, Little Rock should not, it seemed to me, have been compared to New York or Washington, but to cities of like size and economy: cities such as Wichita, Kansas; Des Moines, Iowa; or Louisville, Kentucky.

But in 1955 and 1956, before all of the things that happened did happen, we were only happy that we had a school board and a school superintendent dedicated to the preservation of public schools and to high educational standards in those schools—come what may. We thought it extremely unfortunate that these people, after working so hard to devise a plan which should have eliminated the complaints of the racists (the ones who publicly warned about the dangers of immediate and massive integration) should so soon become the victims of slander and character assassination by the very ones they thought they were appeasing.

As to the potential problems which might have resulted from immediate and complete integration, and about which the White Citizens Council people warned us again and again and again, my wife and I felt we would prefer to have our children run these alleged risks than to run the risk of becoming bigoted and prejudiced. Beyond that, we did not want them to believe that you can disregard a court order if you can just stir up sufficient mob action. To me, one of the most disgusting spectacles seen through the two or three years of the school crisis in Little Rock was that of a congressman's wife at the state capital giving the "marchers" a pep talk as the high schools reopened on an integrated basis in the fall of 1959.

But mainly, we didn't want our children to get the idea that they were entitled to automatic preferential treatment all through life as a result of something they had nothing to do with. We knew that they would have to prove themselves in equal competition later in life, and felt that they might as well learn while still young. Most important, we thought, they would find a way to put into actual practice the teachings of Christ, which they studied each Sunday.

We were told by several people that there was a different type Negro in Little Rock, different from the Negro we had known in Iowa and other Midwestern states. At first I was willing to accept this idea but later came to the conclusion that there is little basic difference in Americans. I have become acquainted with many fine colored people in Little Rock, people who have displayed qualities of leadership and whose children were well able to handle the curriculum in Little Rock's, or any other American high school. Certainly these colored people and their children have often displayed great courage, considerable restraint, and Christian attitudes that would, or should, put many of their antagonists to shame. But even before these qualities became evident, I could not believe that the colored people of Little Rock were so much more aggressive, unintelligent, or persuasive than colored people in other parts of America.

In any event, it seemed to us that the frequently used segregationist argument that Negroes in their particular city or region are so much less "ready" for integration than they are elsewhere is in reality an indictment against the system of

racial segregation which produced the allegedly culturally inferior Negroes.

When we first arrived in Little Rock, the coming school
integration seemed no more than a small speck on the distant
horizon. It wasn't mentioned a great deal and no one, or so it
seemed then, was particularly concerned. People knew that
the United States Supreme Court had ruled segregated public
schools unconstitutional, and that, to most people, was that.

But even then, we were constantly aware that there was
supposed to be quite a difference in attitudes toward Negroes
in the South from the attitudes we had been used to. Since
then, I have come to the conclusion that prejudice is a natural human tendency, and that it is normally displayed
against racial, national, or religious minorities whenever the
opportunity, or encouragement, presents itself. Prejudice is no
more innate in the southerner than it is in people anywhere.
We remembered, of course, that in many parts of America
Negroes are not present in sufficient numbers to provide the
necessary outlet for feelings of group superiority; so, in such
cases, the prejudice is usually directed toward other minorities, such as Jews, Orientals, or Mexicans; or against Catholics, or even against southerners!

For the first few months we lived in Little Rock I was not
concerned with all the complexities of racial prejudice and
the reasons for it, psychological or sociological, and was content to watch for what I had been led to believe were great
differences in attitudes. About the only real difference discovered was the ability of those inclined toward prejudice to
get an audience or a following. People living in regions where
there is no minority to look down on, and feel superior to,
are no doubt as anxious to belong to the "master race" as
people anywhere, but they look a little silly talking about their
superiority and about a threat to themselves when everyone
knows there is really no problem. So these folks usually fill

their needs, in one way or another, through religious bigotry or by criticism of people just a step down the economic or cultural ladder. Since admission of prejudice does not make one popular in some parts of America, bigoted people in these regions are inclined to keep their ideas to themselves.

But in Little Rock, the people with the basic need for prejudice, the ones who really enjoyed it, were able to find encouragement since there were enough Negroes present to provide the necessary scapegoat. Furthermore, because of the presence of this minority, many members of the clergy, politicians, and employers have exploited, for various reasons, the natural tendencies that people everywhere have for feeling superior, or the desire to belong to a group that is considered superior.

So, although the people in Little Rock have many wonderful qualities, and although we were much impressed with the friendliness, courtesy, and kindness demonstrated by the majority of the people that we came to know as neighbors, friends, and co-workers, we, nevertheless, had a difficult time adjusting to the attitudes of a very vocal group of racists. Unfortunately, these people were seldom discouraged a great deal by others. This was probably to be expected as most Little Rock citizens saw nothing to gain and possibly quite a bit to lose, in becoming "crusaders."

There is probably no single answer to why some people become extremely prejudiced while others do not. No doubt many factors are involved. But it would seem that the degree of prejudice is usually in direct proportion to education or lack of it, to youth or lack of it, and to personal success or lack of it. It would be difficult to apply this yardstick in parts of America where minority groups are not present in great numbers, but even in such states as Iowa, the same causes seem to have the same effects.

In 1958 and 1959 a new expressway was built through a

part of Des Moines occupied primarily by Negroes. Most of them were forced to relocate. The Des Moines *Register* carried several editorials; civic, educational, and religious leaders urged people all over the city to be good neighbors as colored people moved into their neighborhoods. Most people were good neighbors, but there were some incidents. There were "Nigger go home" signs painted on newly purchased homes. So it is obvious that no part of America is immune to bigotry and prejudice. But I think it is important to remember that the people committing lawless acts in Des Moines were the same type of people who were involved in mob action at Central High School. There were few college graduates, business, civic, or religious leaders involved in either group.

We had not lived in Little Rock long before we discovered that many of the people in Arkansas were very liberal in their views on race; but at first we were only aware of the feelings of those with extreme prejudices. This is probably because these people are so much more vocal and emotional about their beliefs than others are. Of course, views considered extreme in Little Rock might well be considered moderate in Mississippi or Alabama, as even the extremists in Little Rock seemed willing to grant others freedom of thought and opinion. The men and women I worked with in my railroad work were probably no more or no less prejudiced than others. Some of them were and are quite liberal, while others seemed to consider race-caste the most important thing in the world. But the discussion of race relations with co-workers usually has taken the form of good-natured kidding and as long as I readily admitted prejudice was nation-wide most of the people I talked to about segregation seemed willing to admit that there were two sides to the question and that change was inevitable. Still, it took quite a while for me to get used to some of the statements, and the apparent beliefs of the more extreme.

I JUST LIKE TO WATCH HIM PLAY BALL

Once, during the tense days in 1957, a fellow worker and I were discussing baseball and the relative merits of some of the better-known stars. When I mentioned an outstanding play by Willie Mays, my friend seemed amazed that I should include the name of this intruder and asked me what I considered a totally irrelevant question: "How," he exploded, "would you like to have your daughter—etc." I had expected this question, but not as a result of a baseball discussion. I answered, "Well, I really didn't want to marry Willie, I just like to watch him play ball!" With talk such as this going on no one in the office could remain very serious, not even the man who had considered Willie's presence in the major leagues a breach of good conduct for Negroes. So everyone wound up laughing about it, as we usually did somewhere along the line. But I did want my friend to know that I wasn't trying to evade a question that seemed crucial to him. So I went on to say that I felt racially mixed marriages would normally not prove successful as long as our society does not permit such unions to be happy. I said that I was sure the vast majority of people, regardless of race, felt this way, too. But I also let my friend know that as far as I was concerned all of this had nothing to do with the denial of rights, opportunity, and justice to a part of our citizenry. I implied that as far as actual mixing of genes was concerned, I had gotten the impression that there had been much of it done, judging from some of the boasts I had heard, by the very people who were so vocal against it.

In addition to the "would you want your daughter" bit, I got all the other timeworn arguments and allegations, one by one.

Two or three times when perspiration-soaked Negroes came

to my office to perform work of one kind or another, I was told
(as soon as the Negroes were out of hearing range) about the
odor supposed to be peculiar to colored people. Since I had
worked alongside a good many perspiration-soaked white men
in my younger days, when I was a railroad section laborer,
I insisted that it was the same old smell, and nothing that
a little Lifebuoy or Dial wouldn't take care of, but I could see
my point was not well taken.

Once when we got the report of a fourteen-year-old girl's
injury (her leg was amputated by a freight train passing
through the city), I was shocked because two or three people
immediately asked, "Was she white?" In accidents involving
Negroes it became obvious that, to the racist, the death of a
Negro was of little consequence. This was hard for me to
get used to, as I had always thought of a human life as a
human life.

Most people in Little Rock who can afford it have Negro
help. These colored people are employed as maids or "yard
boys." We were told by several people that these Negroes
could be expected to remove just about everything from our
property that was "not nailed down," and that they would,
in all likelihood, get drunk frequently and show up only if
they felt like it.

When we decided we were able to afford some part-time
help, I obtained the services of a middle-aged colored woman
whose husband's wages as a cotton picker were not sufficient
to meet the minimum requirements of living. This colored
woman worked for us for some time and we operated as usual.
We left loose change and currency lying around on tables or
dressers. We left watches, jewelry, and other items where we
happened to put them down and never missed a thing. We
were told by some of the neighbors that we were making a
mistake in paying the woman $1.00 an hour when the going
rate was fifty cents, and that we shouldn't "spoil them." But

we came to the same conclusion that you generally get about what you pay for, regardless of color.

When I needed to get some yard work done, instead of hiring one of the older Negroes around town about whom we had heard so many deprecating remarks, I went to the dean of men at Philander Smith College, a school for Negroes in Little Rock sponsored by the Methodist Church, and asked if any of the students wanted part-time work. He sent a young ministerial student with me, who said he planned to enter Michigan State the following year. This colored boy and Carl and I worked together on the yard all day, taking time out to eat lunch and for a Coke now and then. We also played a few games of basketball on our outdoor court. During the games Carl and I were soundly beaten at shooting baskets, although we had previously considered ourselves on a par with Bob Cousy in accuracy. After the colored boy had returned to college that evening, Carl asked me casually, "Dad, what's all this fuss about integration? I don't get it!"

Another argument thrown at me frequently by those I worked with was the one having to do with "states' rights." I wasn't too familiar with the subject; no one in Iowa had ever worried about states' rights, but since I was hearing about it so much I did give it considerable thought. It seemed to me that the only rights the segregationists were really concerned about were the rights they thought they had to treat Negroes as they saw fit without regard to any rights Negroes might have as American citizens. But I knew it would do no good to use this line of reasoning. So I used what seemed to me an appropriate analogy. I told the segregationist railroad employees that I certainly saw nothing wrong with regional pride, such as the pride displayed by most Texans; a pride which is known and at least tolerated by most other Americans. However, I pointed out that there was a lot more to the problem than regional pride, and that I felt there should be a larger pride for the nation than for the state. I went on to say that we knew our railroad was made up of several divisions, each of which was under the immediate supervision of a superintendent, and that we all shared pride in our respective divisions while we jokingly downgraded other divisions. I said further that as long as our division ran smoothly we seldom heard from the president of the road, except for an occasional courtesy call. But we also knew that in policy matters there was but one final authority and that was vested in the president and his staff in Chicago. We knew that if the various superintendents were permitted to countermand the instructions of the president, even though a particular superintendent and his employees might think the president wrong, chaos would be the result. We were aware that years ago our railroad was made up of several smaller companies, but that when they merged there had to be an effective chain of command, and that if this was not formed, and if the chain of command did not function smoothly, our ability to survive would be seriously impaired. I asked my friends what they would think of a division superintendent who would deliberately try to undermine the work of the president of the road, just to enhance his own popularity, at a time the road was fighting for survival. My friends said they wouldn't think much of such a superintendent—but that they didn't see what all this had to do with states' rights!

Most of the strong segregationists that I came in daily contact with at work stressed their apprehension about racially mixed marriages whenever we talked about racial prejudice. Many other aspects of the problem were discussed but the conversations usually ended with sexual overtones. This was not unexpected, and for a time I was convinced that this *was* the primary concern of the strong segregationist.

But I had not been working in Little Rock many years until I became aware that there is something even more terrifying to the racist than fears of interracial marriage.

As mentioned earlier, quite a few of my co-workers enjoyed discussing prejudice and segregation with me, and we did a lot of kidding about it. Everyone knew pretty well how everyone else felt. Some of the employees in my building didn't take the segregation issue very seriously, while others did.

Part of my work for the railroad consists of interviewing prospective employees to screen out the undesirables and to hire those seeming to possess sufficient intelligence and ability to handle various jobs.

One of the railroad's employees seemed particularly fond of discussing segregation with me. He was actually quite liberal in his views and told me (off the record, of course) that he felt pretty much as I did. But he enjoyed needling me about my views, and I am sure he doubted that I really believed some of the things I said.

STIRRING THE HORNETS' NEST

We experienced seasonal shortages of various classes of employees and at one time were having difficulty hiring enough qualified telegraph operators to meet our requirements. Learning telegraphy is not easy, and a good many young men out looking for jobs seemed to feel that they should be able to get good jobs without having to spend from six to eight months in preparation.

It was during one of these shortages of telegraphers that my needling friend breezed into my office grinning like the proverbial cat which had swallowed the canary. With him was a rather frightened-looking colored boy who stood there nervously, hat in hand. My friend introduced the boy, saying that he was originally from a small town in south Arkansas, and that he had spent several months in a telegraph school in Colorado and was anxious to obtain employment. By this time most of the people in the building were aware of what was going on and were anxiously awaiting the outcome. There were looks of amazement, shock, and incredulity as I told the colored boy I would be glad to interview him. I was aware that it was unlikely I could hire him but was willing to try.

The boy did well on the aptitude test and did well in all aspects of the patterned interview. When I concluded the interview I asked the young man if he did not realize he had broken an unwritten law. He smiled slightly and said that he was aware of his misdeed, but that Little Rock was close to his home. He had come home to see his parents and he thought he might as well give it a try and see what happened. I told him I would do what I could and let him know.

When he had gone I checked with the man on our division who had the final authority as to hiring, and he told me he would write for a ruling, saying someone "higher up" would have to make the decision. In a few days a letter came saying it was a local matter and that we would have to make the decision in Little Rock. I asked my boss again, and he said that while he felt as I did, he didn't want to stir up a "hornets' nest," and that he didn't want to be first on the system to hire a Negro telegrapher and asked me if I wanted to be first. I said yes, I did. But I knew that the matter was ended and that he was not going to give me the necessary authority. So I wrote the colored boy and told him I was truly sorry.

I am sure a lot of the employees breathed sighs of relief when they found the color line had not been broken. The whole thing was quite educational to me. Of course, railroads are no different from other industries in their employment practices, and, as a matter of fact, probably hire more Negroes at a higher average wage than most other industries. But the pattern was there. Negroes worked as cooks, waiters, porters, mail handlers, and janitors.[1] But they could not ob-

[1] My company does hire Negroes for clerical positions and for other skilled jobs in Chicago and in other cities on its northern district.

tain a really skilled and responsible job regardless of qualifications.

I asked the boy to let me know if he ever got work as a telegrapher. I doubted that he would and thought it too bad that a telegraph school would take his money under apparently false pretenses, as they did promise the boys jobs upon graduation. But in a few months, I got word that the young man had actually been hired by a terminal railroad in Chicago.

So I think about this every time the segregationists start in on Chicago. I don't doubt that there are some terrible things happening in Chicago, as there are in New York and Philadelphia. And having grown up in a small town, I feel sure I would not enjoy big-city living. I realize that there are flagrant violations of the civil rights of minority groups in these cities. But at the same time I can't help remembering that this colored boy had to go to Chicago to get something very important—a job commensurate with his talent, ability, and desire.

The remarks I heard about my abortive attempt to institute fair employment practices dispelled any illusions I might have had about "mongrelization" or "miscegenation" being the primary fear of the racist.

All of this may give the reader the impression that just about everyone in Little Rock has, or has had, extreme views on the integration issue. This, of course, is not true. A majority of the people in Little Rock, in recent years, have proven that they are quite progressive where race is concerned, as they have rebounded from original outbursts of bigotry in high places and restored Little Rock's reputation as a city of racial good will. But while the so-called moderates remained silent, waiting for some progressive leadership, the racists were given encouragement rather than discouragement by people who should have had more strength of character. They were given encouragement by politicians who hoped to

ride into office using race as a vehicle, by businessmen hoping
to exploit the issue at the expense of their competitors, and
by ministers who learned to depend entirely upon emotion
to get a following.

During our first two years in Little Rock we were impressed
by the willingness of the community to accept changes in
the field of race relations. Railroad waiting rooms, libraries,
buses, and parks had been, or were in the process of being,
desegregated. We heard the coming school integration being
discussed rationally and objectively. It was obvious that most
of the people would have preferred to retain segregated
schools, but they did not expect to. They seemed hopeful
that the transition could be made smoothly. They appeared to
be confident that the school board and the school superintendent's plan would minimize any of the harmful effects supposed to be inevitable because of integration, and about
which many of the racists were starting to make a lot of noise.

We heard a great deal of talk about "outsiders" from the
strong segregationists. So we refrained from saying much at
the outset of Little Rock's travail. One of the things that led
us to believe that there were more extremists than there actually were was the large numbers of "Letters to the Editor"
which were being published in both Little Rock daily newspapers, and particularly in the *Arkansas Democrat*. The
letters published usually were more than derogatory about Negroes, and they always attempted to cast doubt on the integrity or patriotism of all who dared to disagree with the writers.
These letters seemed to get particularly caustic when national
leaders were discussed. By now we have discovered that the
same twenty-five or thirty people write nearly all of these letters, but at first it seemed that there was an endless stream of
them. One of these would-be Hemingways, an extremely
vocal segregationist from the town of Delight, Arkansas, had
letters published in the *Democrat* five consecutive days during one of his more prolific outbursts of letter writing. We

found out, before long, that liberals normally don't write these letters to the editor, or indulge in anonymous, threatening phone calls to people they disagree with. One liberal told me later that he had written a letter once, for publication, but that he subsequently happened to notice an inscription on the walls of a public comfort station reading, "Fools' names and fools' faces are often seen in public places," and that he hadn't written a letter to the editor since.

CARPETBAGGERS FROM THE SOUTH

Anyway, with all this reference to outsiders, we could see that the advocates of local self-government had a following. But we were amazed, in the summer of 1957, to see outsiders take over, after all! Furthermore, they seemed to be welcomed enthusiastically by all members of the same organizations who had talked so much about outsiders. These modern-day carpetbaggers did not come from the North, though. Rather, they came from some of the Deep South states and were sent by organizations who also claimed to be strong advocates of "local self-government." They poured in from far and near, threatening, cajoling, lamenting, beseeching, and placing advertisements in the newspapers (in those newspapers which did not consider the material to be in poor taste). Nearly all of these advertisements, for which the racist groups seemed to have unlimited funds, were designed to insult or humiliate the Negro, or, at the very least, to create the impression that the government of the United States of America was the enemy of the people. Many of the notices sought to convince the people of Little Rock that our own school board, city officials, and some of our ministers were of doubtful integrity. They attempted to cast doubt on any of the leaders in the community who dared to take a stand for law against lawlessness, for reason against unreasonableness, and for compassion against hate. Seven years later we cannot help but recall that many of these outsiders came from cities which have since desegregated with a good deal more calmness than they recommended for us.

Those of us who watched these invasions can be a little bit sympathetic with the Governor, who apparently decided that if he couldn't lick 'em, he might as well "jine 'em."

For some time after the crisis of 1957 and 1958, we wondered if things would ever get back to normal. Each time tempers seemed to cool, the Governor seemed to get wind of some new and sinister threat to our "way of life." These tips, he told us, came from "a very reliable source." But he told the faithful that they should continue to "keep the faith," and that he had a plan which would solve everything; that the schools would soon reopen on a segregated basis, and that everything would go on just as before.

Eventually, it became quite clear even to the adamant that the only thing the Governor could really do was to issue press releases and keep emotions at a high pitch. We began to wonder why we should continue to remain silent, as outsiders. We were *not* outsiders. We were residents of Little Rock and of Arkansas and had a stake in the future of both. We had every reason to be interested in the Little Rock school system and in the industrial growth of the city and state. It seemed to us that the real outsiders were the ones who kept coming into Little Rock trying to convince the people of Little Rock that it would be better to shut down our schools than to make any effort to comply with court orders pertaining to desegregation.

Even though we finally decided to take a firm stand on the desegregation issue, we continued to experience utter frustration for some time. We watched Governor Faubus as he ran for a third term, as he allegelly polled the people and said he found 85 per cent of the people were with him, then went out and campaigned using the slogan, "It's courage that counts."

We wished desperately that there was something we could do to help restore reason, but at the time it seemed quite hopeless. We felt that if we could help to reopen the schools, and help offset one of the most brazen displays of demagoguery seen in recent years, we could do our part in letting the world know that it had gotten a distorted picture of Little Rock and its people. But voices like ours were seldom heard and rarely listened to in Little Rock in 1957 and 1958.

A few of the churches in Little Rock, in 1957, had preachers who preached against race hatred and prejudice. Youngsters from these churches quite often reflected the teachings of their ministers in their public statements and in their treatment of Negroes. But in many cases the white youngsters who were courageous enough to speak out against racism were subjected to nearly as much harassment as were the Negroes.

With such things going on, it would have been logical to assume that the religious leadership in the rest of the community would have something to say. But they were strangely silent. All they'd have had to do would have been to recommend the Golden Rule for their kids. But they said nothing.

In talking to preachers since that time I have tried to find out why they did not give help to the young people in their own congregations, who so desperately needed it. I asked why they did not say something to the kids who had been led to believe that beatings, spitting, threats, and cursing were the proper way to preserve a way of life known for its friendliness and courtesy. I also mentioned the obscene pamphlets and cards passed out periodically by some of the white students, but which had been made available by adults—the same adults who pretended to be worried about the morals of their children.

I was told that the matter was so controversial that bringing it up might endanger the Lord's work.

During the school crisis a group of the larger churches in

Little Rock joined together to sponsor a city-wide prayer meeting to ask for divine guidance and to ask that God's will be done. But they were careful to avoid pointing out specific examples of race prejudice and hatred. When this prayer meeting was announced, a group of segregationist preachers announced a rival prayer meeting. At this meeting they prayed that God would send the "niggers" back to their own schools, where they belonged. They did not make the request that "God's will be done," I noticed, probably being fearful that God's will conceivably might not concur with their own.

After the mob action had occurred in front of Central High School, a segregationist lawyer defended the mob for its action, saying that these "patriots" had only been exercising their constitutional rights of freedom of speech and assembly. A segregationist preacher also defended the mob in statements to the press. He placed advertisements in the *Arkansas Democrat* at frequent intervals, seeking to reveal that much of the clergy was hypocritical on the subject of segregation (which it was), or how the clergy had become infiltrated with communists, or had gotten "soft" on integration. He also tried to get in a few licks at local civic leaders who were trying to solve what had become a difficult problem. More often, he struck out at national leaders and usually ended with a plea for a few dollars to help him in his fight against "Godless Communism" and "race-mixing."

THE "RACE-MIXING" BUSINESS

The term "race-mixing" is one that has never been explained to me, despite all the other "explanations" received from segregationist friends. I find that Negroes can be in our best restaurants mopping the floors, preparing the food, carrying out the dishes, or involved in other menial tasks, and no one objects, even though they may be found throughout the establishment; but this is not "mixing"! However, if a lone Negro should sit down at a lunch counter in a department store to order a cup of coffee, then he has mixed.

Negroes can wander about the rail and bus stations, rubbing elbows with all the staunch segregationists, but as long as they are pushing a broom, carrying grips, or shining shoes, they are not mixing. But the minute one of them puts down his broom and gets ready to board a train or bus, he must not occupy the same waiting room, or he has mixed.

Negroes can come to your home and work all day, take care of your children while you are gone, and that's not mixing. But if one of your maid's children dares to enroll in the same high school with your children, then they are guilty of the crime of mixing.

If you ride up or down on an elevator crowded with people of both races, of all shapes and sizes, oddly enough that's not mixing. And there is no objection to working side by side with Negroes, if they are doing janitor work or are classed as helpers. But if a Negro has the audacity to apply for a skilled job, even as a telegrapher where he would likely to be sent to a one-man station with little chance to mix with anyone, he would then be accused of mixing.

Ah, well, I guess, as some of the segregationists say of me, I just don't understand them. Which reminds me of the story about the chorus girl out with a well-to-do business man. When she asked him, sympathetically, "What's the matter, honey, doesn't your wife understand you?" he replied, sourly, "My problem is, she understands me too well!"

In the fall of 1958, the Little Rock public high schools were closed and it was necessary to send Carl to a private school hurriedly set up by the Baptist churches of the city. The people operating the school did the very best they could to provide schooling, but the education received could not remotely resemble the education received in Little Rock's fine system of public high schools. For example, in one of Carl's classes, three instructors either resigned or were dismissed within a three-month period. For this substandard schooling we were charged a tuition of $25 per month and it was this low because all facilities were donated by churches. But it developed that the $25 tuition did not cover other expenses. So we were asked for further contributions. And all this was in addition to the taxes we were paying for the fine public high schools we were not permitted to use.

In the spring of 1959 the people finally rebelled. This happened when the die-hard segregationists on the school board attempted to discharge about fifty of the oldest and most respected of the city's public schoolteachers, on the grounds that they were soft on integration. (One was reported to have made the statement that she believed the colored students should be treated as she would want to be treated if the situation were reversed.) According to the Arkansas law at that time, a special election could be held to recall school-board members not wanted by the patrons of the school district. The law had been enacted to enable patrons to throw out school-board members suspected of being sympathetic to desegregation, or, for that matter, for being suspected of being sympathetic only to those Negro students being subjected to the cruelest forms of harassment. But the whole scheme backfired. The group under the S.T.O.P. banner ("Stop This Outrageous Purge") obtained sufficient signatures to force a special recall election. A rival group, hastily formed by segregationists, quickly got to work. They called themselves the Committee to Retain Our Segregated Schools (C.R.O.S.S.). I thought it particularly sickening for a group dedicated to the denial of equal citizenship rights for Negroes to brazenly take a name symbolizing love. (Maybe this had something to do with their defeat at the polls.) As a result of this special election, racists on the school board were replaced by men describing themselves as moderates. Little Rock's public high schools reopened in 1959.

But in the fall of 1959 there was no assurance that there would be any end to our continuing crises! Even though the kids were back in school, politicians still seemed unwilling to play down, rather than play up, racial tension.

Chapter 5

TRYING TO BE REALISTIC ABOUT THE GOVERNOR

Many writers these days seem to have a one-track mind—track sex! Now I have nothing against sex and feel that it is here to stay. But there are other aspects to life. So it seems unfortunate that we often have the idea a book must feature sex in order to reach a lot of people. There is no question that this gimmick has been used to sell many things. Authors sometimes insert a little sex just to attract the reader so they can get their main points across.

I considered this and wondered if I should try to utilize the sensual on the theory that the end justifies the means. But I am an exponent of the idea that evil means should never be used to acquire just ends. So, dear reader, I must warn you that if you expect to find something in this book that will appeal to your animal nature, you are doomed to disappointment.

It would be difficult to write a book about race prejudice and about Little Rock without discussing Mr. Faubus. I certainly do not intend to try. My appraisal of him may not satisfy those who picture him as another Hitler, since I stress some of his liberal tendencies. But I think it important to be fair and objective.

The study of Governor Faubus is important, not because

Faubus himself is important but because men such as he in American political life have, for many years, kept our republic from functioning as effectively and as beneficially as it should have. A study of the words and actions of a man who could be considered an "old pro" in the field should be worthwhile.

Mr. Faubus certainly is not going to leave any impressive footprints on the sands of time. He was not the first politician to exploit social unrest and won't be the last. But he has been one of the most effective.

A lot of my liberal friends do considerable fretting about our Governor's long tenure in office. But I think they sometimes fail to remember what it might have been like if we'd had to put up with a *real* racist. And while I personally would have preferred a governor like Terry Sanford of North Carolina or Bert Combs of Kentucky, I try to be realistic about the matter and look at the bright side. In addition to the fact that things could have been a lot worse, the political situation as it has developed in Arkansas has given us liberals something to talk about and joke about, in our social gatherings. To us, many of the words and actions of Governor Faubus and some other governers are far more ridiculous than mistakes made by uneducated and economically handicapped Negroes. So I have urged my liberal friends to relax and enjoy the show. There are even crude jokes that some tell to offset the race-based jokes which are the forte of the segregationists. For example, there is the story of the Negro truck driver, in a Deep South state, poking along the highway with a load of chickens, at well below the minimum authorized speed. A state policeman signaled the offender to the shoulder of the road and demanded, "What's the matter with you, boy? You got a governor in that truck?" Scratching his head, the driver finally replied, sniffing the air, "Naw, sir, boss, that's them chickens you smell."

Now since I try to discourage the telling of crude jokes by

racists, I naturally discourage equally crude jokes by liberals. There are plenty of things to laugh about when you watch the maneuvers of demagogic politicians and their followers without resorting to such tactics.

WHEN FAUBUS WAS THE LIBERAL

In the 1956 campaign, the Governor's opponent was an avowed racist, and in this contest Mr. Faubus was the liberal. In a telecast, the Governor held up, for all to see, pictures showing white girls dancing with Negro men. Mr. Faubus said that his opponent had been using these faked pictures in an effort to smear him. Mr. Faubus asked the people if they would want a man for governor who would deliberately stir up racial hatred by such methods. The people certainly did not, and they re-elected the Governor for his second term. Not many months later Mr. Faubus again took to television, and again held up pictures. These photographs showed some mean looking paratroopers poking bayonets at innocent high school girls' posteriors. Upon close scrutiny it was quite plain to see that the girls thought the whole business quite funny, but these facial expressions were difficult to catch on the television screen. Anyway, Mr. Faubus implied in his speech that he thought things had come to a pretty pass when innocent high school girls had to suffer such highhanded treatment. In a later TV speech, when campaigning for certain school-board members, the Governor sorrowfully told the viewers that the Little Rock schools would be integrated only over his prostrate form. Then, a few months after that, when Little Rock's private school folded up for lack of funds, the Governor, still very much erect physically, didn't lift a finger to put the private schools back in business.

In the spring of 1962 Governor Faubus bought television time to explain to the faithful that he was retiring from the political scene. During the first part of the show the Governor, brushing a tear from his eye, read a letter from a little old lady who was telling him that if he wasn't around to make sure she got her monthly welfare check, all was lost. Nevertheless, Orval said, he must step aside. Not many days later the Governor revealed that he had gotten so much mail from people insisting that he run again, that there had been so much pressure, and that his arm had been twisted so badly, he simply must respect this mandate from the people and serve one more time.

In his "final" dramatic telecast, just prior to his being "drafted" for a fifth term, the Governor had some things to say about the editor of the *Arkansas Baptist Newsmagazine*. This may have been because the editor had questioned, editorially, the Governor's exploitation of the race issue. So in closing his "final" speech, the Governor said he would pray that the editor would be "saved" before Faubus someday, in the distant future, decided to re-enter politics.

Now, Faubus himself is a Baptist (there is nothing I can do about it) and we Baptists ordinarily don't treat the question of salvation lightly. We believe that once we are given eternal life, it cannot be taken away from us.

As you may have gathered from what has gone before, I have no objections to looking for the humorous in the Bible. It seems likely that many of the people mentioned in Bible stories were as human as we are, subject to the same frailties, and likely to get into some humorous situations; and, as so many preachers are wont to say, "Christ wouldn't want us going around with a long face all the time." I'll buy this, but at the same time there are some things that must be considered sacred, and setting ourselves up as judges about others' salvation gets beyond what the Governor described in his speech as "the lighter side."

In most of his campaigns, the Governor did not run particularly hard against his listed opponents. Mostly, he ran

against the *Arkansas Gazette*, the government of the United
States of America, and Daisy Bates. Mrs. Bates headed the
Arkansas branch of the National Association for the Advancement of Colored People. In one of his speeches Mr. Faubus
made it quite plain that he considered Daisy pretty much
responsible for the whole mess. But again, a few months later,
when Mrs. Bates went to call on the Governor, he was most
cordial, and posed for photographers while giving Daisy the
glad hand of friendship.

To me, one of the most amazing talents of Governor
Faubus is his ability to "work both sides of the street." Dis-
interested observers might think that he does nothing to cul-
tivate the Negro vote, but such is not the case. At campaign
time he has Negro workers traveling the state, going into
Negro communities and telling the people the Governor is
not really against integration but that he just says the things
he does to get elected, and he "sure can't do you any good if
he don't get elected!"

In his public statements quoted in the *Arkansas Gazette*
and the *Arkansas Democrat*, Faubus blames the "hard-core
integrationists" for the desegregation of public places in Little
Rock. He blamed it on former Governor Sid McMath and
various other unnamed sinister opponents. But *Jet* magazine,
which I am sure is read by few of the Governor's segregationist followers but by many Negroes, came out with the following item June 20, 1963 (page 12): "Arkansas Gov. Orval E.
Faubus tells friends he intends to make Little Rock the most
integrated city in the South, and without violence. Already,
he has used his influence to begin the desegregation of hotels,
theatres, and restaurants in the capital town. Now he's asking Rep. Wilbur Mills to back a Southern regional plan to
raise the income of families in seven states."

The Governor's ability to make both sides happy borders
on the incredible. As Father Divine used to say, "Peace—it's
wonderful!"

Those outside Arkansas may have been impressed by Governor Faubus' five consecutive terms in office and by his apparent invincibility. To me the amazing thing about it all is that he does not get even more votes than he does. There are many thousands of state employees in Little Rock and each one of them is an automatic vote for Faubus. Many of these make all-out efforts to solicit the votes of their friends and relatives. For example, just before the election in 1960, I asked a lady railroad worker who had seemed anti-Faubus whom she planned to vote for. She rather sheepishly admitted that she was going to vote for Faubus. She said that she had a very good friend who worked for the state and had promised her friend that she would vote for the Governor, in order to insure the continued employment of said friend. The lady told me that she would vote against Faubus if she thought it would do any good, but that his re-election was a foregone conclusion, and so she might as well make this small gesture of good will.

DIDN'T COME TO THINK, BUT TO HOLLER

By now the Governor has such a financially powerful political machine that the extravaganzas put on during each campaign make Colonel LeBlanc's former "Hadacol" carnivals (which made a multimillion business out of selling a patented medicine containing a good percentage of alcohol) look like small potatoes. Huge "Faubus for Governor" caravans roll over the state each two years. These tactics are particularly successful in the rural areas of the state since the small towns are now assured a carnival at least biannually. (Boy, wouldn't Monroe, Iowa, have loved this!) A friend who attended one of these rallies said that he sought out a bona fide local resident (which was rather difficult because of the large number of state employees present) and asked the question, "Well, what did you think of the Governor's speech?" and got the reply, "I didn't come here to think, I came here to holler!"

University of Arkansas football stars sometimes wind up on the campaign trail, plugging for the Governor, and Arkansas beauty contest winners frequently wind up in the Faubus camp.

Young men with political aspirations, those who would normally throw their hat in the ring and make the run for governor, have about reached the point where they are unable, financially, to compete with the Governor's unlimited expense account.

But in spite of all this, in 1962, Governor Faubus polled only slightly more than 51 per cent of the votes cast in Arkansas. He does not get a majority of the votes in Little Rock, a city which has the bulk of the state workers, automatically voting for him, but a city which has had most of the traumatic experiences resulting from his handiwork.

Only 51 per cent of the vote! I regard this as a minor miracle.

Distinguished visitors coming to Arkansas are nearly always impressed by the Governor's warm and friendly personality. When with visitors known to be sympathetic to the Negro's aims, and to visitors from foreign lands, Mr. Faubus usually mentions that there are Negroes in Arkansas holding good jobs, some working for the state. He says he makes appointment without regard to race, creed, or color. He points out the considerable progress Arkansas made in desegregating its public places.

To offset these gestures of liberalism, the Governor has had to drop a few crumbs from his table to some of the more vocal racists in the area. When it appeared the extreme segregationists on the Little Rock school board would be recalled, the Governor appeared on television to blast the hard-core integrationists in Little Rock, and also the schoolteachers who had been accused of softness on integration (such as advocating the practice of the Golden Rule when dealing with Negro students).

A lot has been said about former Little Rock School Superintendent Virgil Blossom. He was looked upon as a champion of moderation—or of integration, depending on where you sat. Actually, some of the schoolteachers have said that it was Blossom's idea for the schools to go ahead and comply with the minimum requirements of the courts, but that when the few Negro children showed up they would not be "welcome" and would return to Negro schools. Then the schools would be technically desegregated, but still all white, or all Negro—all nice and legal. But Governor Faubus spoiled all of this by forcing a showdown and making it a real challenge. Since Little Rock is looked upon as a turning point for the entire South, this whole theory, while still nothing but theory, is indeed something to think about.

I was told by several people that Mr. Faubus is a very personable fellow and a joy to know. A friend of mine put it to me this way: "If Faubus were in the same room with you for ten minutes, he'd have your vote." I found later that my friend was right, as this same friend introduced me to the Governor at a gridiron banquet. Mr. Faubus complimented me on my writing, and I'd certainly have to admit that he was a mighty congenial fellow.

MOST SINCERELY, ORVAL E. FAUBUS

In the little book Carl and I wrote about race prejudice we said several things about Governor Faubus that were hardly complimentary. For example, in discussing the desegregation of public schools we said: "Several other states, with attitudes similar to those found in Arkansas, such as Virginia, North

Carolina and Oklahoma, have adopted varying degrees of school integration unaccompanied by racial incidents in or near the schools. But it should be remembered that in each of these states, the students, the school boards, the law enforcement agencies and the general public had the support and cooperation of their governors, once it was seen that desegregation would be necessary for public schooling to continue. They were encouraged by their governors to prove their good citizenship. We had to prove ours the hard way!"[1]

There were other, similar references, to Governor Faubus' handiwork. So I could never understand why the Governor did not seem to be offended. But, in looking back, I can see that the book hardly scratched the surface, and that few, if any, of the Governor's segregationist followers had read the book. I suspect he felt the less said, the better.

In the summer of 1961 I was invited to appear on a New York television show to talk about our book and about Little Rock. I wrote Mr. Faubus, after sending him a complimentary copy of our book, and asked for a short interview so that I might be better prepared for my TV appearance. Mr. Faubus answered promptly, declining to give me an interview. He said that because of a multitude of special legislative problems he could not spare the time. He said that the subject with which I dealt could not be treated "hastily or lightly" and that this was about all that could be accomplished in what would have to be a brief interview.

But the surprising thing about his letter was how much it sounded like other letters I had received from Senators Douglas and Humphrey. In his letter the Governor pointed out that his efforts as governor had been directed toward all people in the state, regardless of section, station in life, creed, or color. He said that he had made appointments without regard to the differences mentioned above. He did say that

[1] *This Is What We Found*, page 55.

he felt some of our problems could be solved only by "evolution and education."

After I read his letter I told my wife that I had not realized how really liberal our great Governor was. I told her I almost felt like sitting down and writing him a letter saying, "Keep up the good work, pal, you work on the evolution, I'll work on the education, and between us we'll whip bigotry and prejudice yet!"

Two years later I wrote an article about race-based hypocrisy in many of our churches. In the article I mentioned the Governor's standing to join in an ovation for a speaker who had concluded his remarks with the statement, "You and I will not be free, until James Meredith is free!"

This time I got a letter from the Governor which was not so cordial. My article was published in the *Arkansas Gazette*, the *Arkansas Baptist*, and other state papers, and probably reached two or three hundred thousand people. I rather think the Governor did not care to have his segregationist supporters reading about his enthusiasm for Mr. Meredith.

In his second letter Mr. Faubus told me that I might be wrong when I called people racists. (I certainly would like to be wrong about this.) He said that I seemed to grant others the right to their opinions, but then condemned them for having those opinions. He said he thought it strange that we integrationists wanted other people to adopt practices that we ourselves refuse to adopt. The Governor also said that while he believed everyone was entitled to equal rights that he did not believe this to include the right to "impose their persons upon others" by federal court order, or otherwise.

But the real clincher was the inclusion of something he usually reserves for special political speeches, when he thinks the going might be a little rough. He suggested that later, when I looked into the sweet innocent faces of my innocent grandchildren, I should write him and tell him if I still considered myself to be "total integrationist."

Well, it was obvious to me that the Governor likes to write, as I do. We could become pen pals, I thought happily! I felt that an answer was indicated. It reads as follows:

"Dear Governor, Thank you for your good letter of April 26th. I was a little puzzled, though, because in the letter you seemed quite critical, although in my article I had attempted to praise you. On the other hand, when you wrote me about my book THIS IS WHAT WE FOUND, which was quite caustic, your letter sounded as though it might have been written by Senator Humphrey.

"You stated a few facts for my consideration. Now let me state some for yours. You said that I accused people of being 'racists.' I singled no one out as being a 'racist,' certainly not you, as I do not consider you one.

"You said you believed everyone is equal in the sight of God. So do I! And if this attitude is good enough for God, then who am I to act differently? At least I should try to follow the teachings of God, and his Son, insofar as I am able.

"You continued by saying that equal rights does not include the right to impose one's person upon another. I am not quite clear as to what you mean by this. I, for example, might not wish to fraternize with certain Methodists, horse-players, segregationists, or Negroes. But I certainly would not feel that I had the right to keep any of these people out of places of public accommodation, or restrict their job opportunities. None of the Negroes I know are trying to impose their 'person' on anyone. They just want an even break.

"I managed to maintain a serious attitude as I read through your letter until I came to the part about looking into the faces of my innocent grandchildren. Really, Governor, I would have expected you to save this for your next 'final' telecast, just prior to being 'drafted' for a sixth term, since many of your followers love this sort of thing. But I cannot take it seriously, and I'll bet you can't either. I can visualize my innocent grand-daughter now, in 1973, as she looks at me incredulously, and says, 'Grandpa, I read in the *Arkansas States-man*[2] that there IS a Santa Claus and that just because I was born into a certain group, I will get an automatic advantage over certain other Americans, and that I can look down on them, and ridicule them because of this, and that they can work twice as hard as I, but still not attain my station in life. But, Grandpa, you said this wasn't so. Tell me, is there a Santa Claus?'

"And I will have to answer and say, 'No, Virginia, I think it only fair to tell you, while you are yet young, that there is no Santa Claus. Just because Governor Faubus says it is so, doesn't make it so. You are going to have to prove your own worth, in competition with ALL other Americans. You won't have an automatic advantage. I think it better to know this while you are still able to adjust. I think you will want it this way, after you think about it. There isn't a great deal of satisfaction to winning when the contest is 'rigged,' is there?'

"Seriously, Governor, I do appreciate your many talents, and your efforts to defend the rights of all the people, regardless of their race, creed, color, or station in life. I am happy that you do not intend to wander in the 'thickets of extremism.' I know there are things you must say, and do, to be elected. But we liberals (integrationists) know that we could have had a governor much less sympathetic to our aims than you have been. We are not entirely ungrateful, even though it may seem that way at times.

"Most sincerely, Ralph Creger"

THE MISTAKE OF APPEALING TO REASON

When Harry Ashmore was editor of the *Arkansas Gazette* he gave the Governor about as much trouble as anyone I know. But although Mr. Ashmore was a brilliant editor and

[2] The weekly paper published by Governor Faubus.

writer, he made the mistake of trying to appeal to reason rather than emotion. He kept trying to give the people facts, when they were not interested in facts. Arkansans were tired of criticism from other parts of America. It wasn't so much the race issue as just being constantly criticized in the nation's press, which put so many on the defensive. But suddenly we had a great champion, our "great Governor" was telling a lot of people where to get off. He even had the President worried! Many felt our knight in shining armor could do no wrong. If some of the rest of us just couldn't agree with our knight, the majority seemed to feel that what he was doing was a small price to pay for the recognition we were getting.

Harry Ashmore recognized the Governor's psychological appeal, and pointed this out in his writing; but the people were not buying. In spite of his many brilliant deductions, Ashmore made the same mistake so many others did. He underestimated the talents of Orval E. Faubus. After the Governor's slate of school-board members was defeated in the special recall election of 1959, Mr. Ashmore was quoted in *Life* magazine as saying that Orval Faubus would never again be able to sit easily upon the back of the tiger he had chosen to ride. The Pulitzer-prize-winning editor went on to say that once Mr. Faubus began to turn from his extreme position, the extreme segregationists would then direct their hate and wrath toward him. But nothing of the sort happened. Orval continued to jog along as easily as always, and even had the tiger purring like a kitten.[3] Every time race relations became

[3] It should be pointed out to those not familiar with Arkansas politics that although Governor Faubus has been highly successful in getting himself elected, "again, and again, and again," he has not had a similar success in getting his legislation passed since the now famous S.T.O.P. school-board election in 1959. Nearly every piece of race-related legislation—or amendment—has been defeated since 1959, particularly those put to popular vote.

too tranquil and the "segregationists" got worried about it, the Governor would take to television and make a speech. Or he would issue a press release, stating that if there was trouble when the golf courses were integrated, he'd be there. "You won't find me running," he'd say. Or he'd make a speech at one of the rural schools, and refer to the "U. S. Supreme School Board" and cause everyone to laugh and applaud. So then the "segregationists" could lean back and relax, everything was under control. "Big Brother" was looking out for them.

They still didn't realize they had been conned. I feel sure that they never will. However, some of the leadership of the extremists have not been so gullible. The White Citizens Council had their boys picketing Little Rock's first integrated baseball game in 1963 with signs reading, "Governor Faubus Plays Ball with Negroes."

Personally, I believe Orval Faubus has great political talent. It seems a pity it could not have been used in a more constructive manner. So if I, who deeply regret some of the things the Governor has done to Arkansas, have such a high regard for his many talents, it's small wonder that those who have approved of his actions think of him as another Lincoln. And he might well be even shrewder than Lincoln, for Lincoln mistakenly said, "You cannot fool all of the people all of the time."

Chapter 6

HUMOR IN THE PULPIT

There are many methods of combating bigotry and prejudice. It has been our experience that persuasion through religion is one of the most effective. Unfortunately, it is employed infrequently. Racists tell us, "You can't legislate social problems." And this is true. Laws and education can help, but most of the people I know who have demonstrated a real change of heart about prejudice have done so because of their religious convictions. The plea to follow Christ's teachings in our relationship with others takes on added significance because the part of our nation with the largest concentration of Negroes is also the region known as the Bible Belt.

One of the easiest ways to hurt someone and treat him as you would definitely *not* want to be treated is to ridicule him, either to his face or behind his back. But ridiculing Negroes is one of the favorite indoor sports of many white people— members of the clergy not excluded. Having to listen to these constant attacks upon people usually not around to defend themselves is one of the reasons we became crusaders.

In our original efforts to help reopen the Little Rock high schools, which eventually involved us in the whole broad field of human rights, we certainly did not think of ourselves as crusaders. It would have been a great deal easier to have ignored what was going on, as so many did, and continue the easy, pleasant living to which we had become accustomed.[1] But because of Carl's chance classroom assignment we did become crusaders—extremists, if you prefer.

We extremists who work for, rather than against, equal human rights, are usually not as vocal as the extremists at the other end of the line. But I think we are no less dedicated. People willing to take stands for causes that are unpopular at the moment and to risk loss of money, popularity, and even close friendships have to be dedicated. The only rewards we can reasonably expect are clear consciences and the feeling that we have been true to ourselves and to our God.

We may have handicapped ourselves because we refuse to adopt many of the tactics used by the opposition. We normally don't make anonymous telephone calls or write threatening letters to those who do not agree with us. We do not subscribe to the theory that the "end justifies the means," and since we like to consider ourselves fair and tolerant, we feel we must extend this fairness and tolerance to our adversaries. This is a courtesy they rarely extend to us.

But I think we must remember that this is a real battle in which we are engaged, and that in battle it is well to capitalize on the weaknesses of your opponent and to attack the enemy at his most vulnerable spot. This is what I have tried to do.

It seems to me that in the Bible Belt we should exploit the weakness of the segregationist's argument at every opportunity. We should not permit the racist to generalize or to ignore the issue as it relates to Christian teachings, from our pulpits, in our Sunday school classes or in Bible studies. We have permitted these people, who have broken the First Commandment by making race-caste their God to take the initiative and to twist and pervert the Bible and Christ's teachings in their hope to perpetuate racial segregation and

[1] We were pleasantly surprised upon finding that we could continue to have the time and the opportunity for the pleasant living.

discrimination. Many of these people are sincere and mean well. But others know better; and the taking of scripture verses out of context, the deliberate misinterpretation of these scripture verses and the use of Christ's name to perpetuate a system in which the worst thing you can be called is a "nigger lover"[2] or a "do-gooder" strikes me as being the ultimate in sacrilege. Surely all this deserves to be exposed and possibly the best way to expose it is to tell some of the things that go on in so many of our churches in regions where racial segregation is practiced.

Some may think the language I use and the stories I tell are in poor taste. They may be, but I feel they are better than double talk and hypocrisy and I think it important that some of these things be said—at long last!

What I have to say, I say because I have become sick at heart at so many of the things I have seen, heard and felt in various churches and in church-related organizations. Some of the things I have witnessed have almost overwhelmed me and caused a cynicism that at times was hard to overcome, until I realized I could not blame Christ because men do not always have the courage to put His teachings into actual practice.

I'M A FUNDAMENTALIST

Most of the churches and the preachers who encourage racists and bigots seem to fall into the fundamentalist category. They like to imply that only religious liberals oppose segregation and work for equal rights. Nothing could be farther from the truth, and, personally, I resent their implications very much.

---

[2] One wonders how Christ, the "Samaritan lover," would be classified in some circles today.

I don't know just what it takes to make one a fundamental-ist, but I have always considered myself one. At least I sub-scribe to all the important doctrines that fundamentalists usually stress. As you have no doubt gathered, I was taught a literal interpretation of the Bible. I believe that the Bible is the inspired word of God. I believe that man does not merit eternal life, but may have this gift by the acceptance of God's Son, Jesus Christ, as Lord and Savior. I believe that Christ was born of a virgin, that He lived a sinless life, was crucified and rose from the dead so that those of us who choose to follow Him and do His will might have eternal life. I think that some of these days He will return to earth, "in like manner" as His disciples saw Him go. In short, I subscribe to all the "fundamental" truths found in the Bible. But some religious groups, as I pointed out, get to the place where they attach more importance to being their particular brand of fundamentalist than they do to being a Christian, and it is with these people that I part company. It is these same people (in regions where they can exploit it) for the most part, who have attempted to "integrate" their theories on race into the Holy Bible.

All my life, in churches throughout the Midwest and the South, I have been going to fundamentalist churches. Preach-ers in these churches will tell you over and over that the way of life they teach is not easy, that you may have to take the unpopular position if you follow Christ. They go on to say that you have to give up certain things, such as card playing, cigarettes, dancing, and movie attendance. They tell you again and again that when you follow Christ you may not be popu-lar "with the crowd," but this will be rewarded by obtaining "peace of mind," "real peace," etc. They tell you it takes real courage to make sacrifices such as this. But many of these same preachers never indicate that it might be well to give up the sin of race hatred and race prejudice, although *this* might entail loss of popularity. When it comes to a real sacrifice, these men of God don't have the courage to ask it of their congregations, and they don't have the courage to make it themselves. Although they pride themselves on their willingness to take the unpopular position, they really only give up the things they knew they were expected to give up when they entered the ministry, and they can't follow through and practice their own preaching when it comes to *their* popularity.

There certainly have been many ministers who have displayed much courage during times of racial crisis. I am sorry to say that all too few have been fundamentalists. There was the Baptist minister in Clinton, Tennessee, who refused to compromise his convictions and defied the people there when they threatened and struck him for his offer of help to Negro children. There was the Methodist minister in New Orleans who refused to take his daughter out of a newly integrated school, despite all sorts of threats and attempted intimidation. There have been many other such examples. Few could be described as fundamentalists. The segregationist-fundamentalist preacher might have been a part of the mob (at the outer edge) and might have been the guiding light of many mob participants; but he seldom opposed the mob in word or deed. He preferred to make his sacrifice by asking his flock to refrain from worldliness, rather than suggest they stop indulging in man's inhumanity to man.

For years I have heard assorted preachers tell about the "brotherhood of man." Of course, the strict fundamentalist will tell you that all men are not brothers, but that only those who have become the "Sons of God" are in reality brothers. I would agree with this, but I certainly find nothing in the Bible to indicate that the Negro cannot become a "joint heir." In fact, we are told that he can: Acts 8:27–31.[3] How-

---

[3] "And he arose and went: and, behold, a man of Ethiopia, a eunuch of great authority under Candace queen of the Ethiopians, who had the charge of all her treasure, and had come to Jerusalem

ever, the segregationist always conveniently overlooks this brotherhood. The ministers tell us that Christian brotherhood should be a common bond between believers, a bond stronger than any other—stronger than the ties of nationality, neighborhood, or politics. They say this, but I feel sure that many of these preachers would rather eat, go to school, share a bus seat, and go to church with a thief, adulterer, embezzler, pervert, or blackmailer who was white than a dedicated, sincere minister of the gospel who happened to be black. This is not my idea of Christian brotherhood and what it should mean.

During the height of the tension in Little Rock, in 1958 and 1959, one of the city's ministers became quite vocal in

---

for to worship, was returning, and sitting in his chariot read Esaias the prophet. Then the Spirit said unto Philip, Go near, and join thyself to this chariot. And Philip ran thither to him, and heard him read the prophet Esaias, and said, Understandest thou what thou readest? And he said, How can I, except some man should guide me? And he desired Philip that he would come up and sit with him. The place of the Scripture which he read was this, He was led as a sheep to the slaughter; and like a lamb dumb before his shearer, so opened he not his mouth: In his humiliation his judgment was taken away: and who shall declare his generation? for his life is taken from the earth. And the eunuch answered Philip, and said, I pray thee, of whom speaketh the prophet this? of himself, or of some other man? Then Philip opened his mouth, and began at the same Scripture, and preached unto him Jesus. And as they went on their way, they came unto a certain water: and the eunuch said, See, here is water; what doth hinder me to be baptized? And Philip said, If thou believest with all thine heart, thou mayest. And he answered and said, I believe that Jesus Christ is the Son of God."

(In addition to the main point of these particular Scripture verses, that of salvation to all, regardless of race or color, I could not help but notice that this particular man was "a man of great authority." He was also obviously trustworthy, well educated and cultured, everything that the racist tells us the Negro is not likely to be. I know of no scripture verses which depict the Negro as being shiftless, dishonest, or uncultured.)

the segregationist movement and at one time ran an advertisement in a Little Rock paper about his church, proudly stating, ALL WHITE CONGREGATION. A friend mentioned this to me and I said we should drive by the church mentioned and see what their bulletin board had to say. We wouldn't have been surprised to have seen the words "Come unto me, all ye white people who are weary, and heavy laden, and I will give you rest."

"NIGRA" STORIES

One of the things that sickened me most during much of Little Rock's tense times was having to listen to the stories, often told from pulpits or on church lawns, in which Negroes were invariably the object of scorn or ridicule.

Most of these stories coming directly from the pulpit were of the more subtle variety, but the point was always clear enough. Other stories, which were sometimes heard in Sunday school classes or at church socials, were a good deal cruder. Here are a few samples:

An old Negro man was asked what organizations he belonged to, and he replied, in proper dialect, "Ah don't belong to nothin' but the Baptist church and the human race, and Ah'm three months delinquent in both of them." This story got one of our revivals off to a rousing start.

More of the same, all told in churches or church-sponsored groups:

A Negro went to heaven and told St. Peter that he had integrated many facilities, such as schools, buses, and libraries. In fact, he said, he had even integrated a Baptist church, which was, he continued, how he happened to have arrived at the pearly gates—as there was no rule specifying how long they could "hold you under."

Of course, to Baptists, baptism is a solemn ordinance, and

one not to be taken lightly—unless the person being baptized should happen to be colored! When Negroes are involved the rules are invariably changed.

Then there's the story of an old Negro who took a trip to Washington. The President invited him to dine in the White House. During the meal the old Negro was asked if he thought he would have been invited to dine with the "white folks" back home. After some hesitation the Negro replied that he guessed he would not, probably because they had a "better class" of white folks back home.

This one is also considered sidesplitting. The first time I heard it I asked innocently about the time Jesus went to dine with Zaccheus, an act for which He was strongly criticized. I asked if perhaps those who criticized Christ would have to be considered a "better class" of people. Those hearing my statement seemed quite shocked.

Once I heard a minister, during his sermon, tell about a colored man who had been away from home for some time, and when he returned he found his wife married to another. In describing his relationship to the newcomer the Negro said he guessed he was his "husband-in-law." This one really got the congregation relaxed and ready for a good sermon on foreign missions. Of course, it belittled the sanctity of marriage, but it was only a story about a Negro, so it didn't matter.

Another funny one made the rounds shortly after a Negro had been taken from a Mississippi jail, killed by a mob, and later found in a nearby river, weighted down by chains. It was said that one of those finding the body, a man who had a particularly good sense of humor, remarked "You'da thought that nigger would knowed better than to try and steal them chains." This one was good for a hearty laugh all around at a social made up of good Christians.

Then there are the stories about "an old colored preacher." These usually originate in the pulpit. They never tell us about the young colored preacher who may have a doctor's degree from a large university, and who may be working untiringly to help his people rise to the cultural level the segregationists say is so lacking. Most of these stories are told in an exaggerated dialect that most modern-day colored ministers could not imitate if they tried. The "Nigra" preachers in the stories are usually well meaning, but obviously stupid individuals, and rather childish and ludicrous. White ministers would resent it deeply if their profession were belittled in this fashion and they were the recipients of the downgrading, but they always seem to think the ministry is funny when Negroes attempt it. When a colored minister does become well known, and if he is obviously intelligent, courageous, and bold, the frightened segregationist immediately accuses him of subversion, agitation, meddling, and all sorts of wrongdoing. He has then "quit preaching and started meddling." It is all right for Negro preachers to preach Christ, but they must never indicate that Christ's teachings are usually not adhered to by white people in their dealings with Negroes.

The racist who also happens to be an active church member, and there are many, always seems to feel that the usual restrictions on conversation and story telling need not apply when the stories are about Negroes. In one group, made up of church people, I heard a story about a new pastor's first sermon in a Negro church. After the sermon he was greeting his new parishoners. One woman was accompanied by three children, and the pastor asked where her husband was. The woman advised that she was unmarried. Then the minister asked who the younger boy belonged to and was told, "He was by the Reverend before you." As to the second oldest, "He was by the Reverend before that." When asked about the oldest child, the woman replied, "Oh, he came along before I became a Christian."

Now to you ministers who would condemn me for the retelling of these stories, I have this to say: You might better advance the kingdom you profess to preach by discouraging the original telling of such stories and by refraining from them yourself. You might tell your flock that when one becomes a follower of Christ he is supposed to become a "new creature," that the old lusts and sins can be overcome provided that there is sufficient faith and dedication, and that the Bible tells us all this and does not except the Negro. You might mention to your congregation that the application of these teachings would help them to eliminate their prejudices and could also change the Negro, as well as the white man. And if they do not believe the applications of Christ's teaching can change the lives of Negroes and eliminate the sins so often complained about, they are demonstrating their lack of confidence that Christ can do what He said He could.

Once in a Bible study group we got into the subject of race, and one woman opined that when Negroes "got religion" they really got it, but that they lost it "just as quick." I remarked, "But I don't understand; I thought we believe 'once saved, always saved.'" The subject was changed!

Now and then you hear a story told by a white preacher that seems to praise the Negro, such as the following: A white minister was visiting in the home of a parishioner. The dinner was served by an old and trusted Negro maid. "Auntie," quipped the minister, "I hope I see you in the next world; I'd hate to think I wouldn't get any more of your good cooking." "Well, Pahson," she answered, "dat depends on you; ah knows where I'se gwine!"

This little anecdote seemed harmless enough, and I suppose it was so intended, but I could not help but think that the real point of the story, whether intentional or not, was, "See here, you superior people, you preach faith, but here was a poor inferior Negro who displayed more faith than any of you. Shame on you, master race."

Chapter 7

SERMONS I'D PREACH

For several years during times of racial tension we sat through sermon after sermon in our own and in other Little Rock churches. We never heard prejudice mentioned until the publication of our first book caused so much comment that our minister finally preached a sermon about the Good Samaritan. He urged us all to be "good neighbors."

But during the time we needed help badly we would never have realized that Little Rock had a serious problem. Certainly we never heard about the spittings, the shovings, the curses, and the jeers that Negro students were subjected to by some of the white students, and by some of their parents, many of whom were, I am sure, professing Christians. The several preachers we heard during the worst of our racial troubles mentioned just about every sin we had ever heard of and a few we had not, except the worst sin man can commit against his fellow man—violation of Christ's second great commandment. Evangelists got very specific about all of the sins they mentioned and described them and their penalties in great detail. But they never denounced the sin of race prejudice nor explained what it might do to men. There were constant pleas to folks to give up the sin which "stood between them and God"—but not one word about giving up prejudice.

In fairness, I must say that all of the preachers we have known, with one exception, agreed that racial prejudice is wrong. They have told us and many other people we know how they felt about it. They just ignored these convictions when delivering their sermons. Still, they at least did not encourage racism. But there were a few preachers in Little Rock who echoed the sentiments of their congregations with vague references to "God being the author of segregation."

We know segregationist preachers think their support of racism is popular with their congregations, and it usually is. But I have been surprised at the number of people ready and anxious for a change in attitude toward Negroes. Usually, young people lead the way. Each generation seems a little less inclined toward bigotry than the one before. But the young people in Little Rock have had help.

Many of my own generation, in our church, were active in helping get the Little Rock schools reopened. They gave evidence in other ways that they were ready for change. One of my close friends, a professional man whose work brings him in contact with Negro men in the same profession, said that it was particularly disturbing to him, after working all morning with a Negro, to be able to go into a nice restaurant and eat lunch, but have to watch his Negro friend carry his meal outside, in a sack. My friend said apologetically (although the situation was certainly not of his making) that this sort of thing was not his idea of what should be going on in a democratic and so-called Christian nation.

Other friends of ours have told us, from time to time, that they admired our stand. Many have done as much as we have in speaking out against racial discrimination. They have spoken from positions of leadership in the church, in the office, and in civic groups. They have done so in Bible study groups, in youth work, and in the Sunday school classroom. But the preachers (when behind their pulpits) have remained silent. At least most of them in Little Rock did, at the time their leadership was needed so very badly. About the only ones who did not remain silent were those catering to their segregationist flocks. They searched through their Bibles trying desperately to find something that would help them in their attempts to justify racial segregation and discrimination.

The fact of the matter is that the Bible has nothing directly to say about segregation or integration of Negroes or of any other peoples. It does have a great deal to say about how *people* should treat *people*. This has provided ample guidance for us.

No doubt many of the Bible-quoting segregationists have spent much time in Bible study, but I have checked the verses they quote and find myself in agreement with Dr. Billy Graham, who says that all of the verses the segregationists quote have to do with the godly remaining "separate" from the ungodly. Dr. Graham makes his position quite clear by refusing to preach to segregated congregations.

It is true that there is ample evidence in the Bible to justify the belief that God would like his followers to avoid becoming "unequally yoked together" with unbelievers. But this is not the sort of segregation that racists want. To them, God ordained segregation, "else why did he put the different races on different continents?" Every time I hear this one I wonder how these people can justify their presence in America. It seems to me they should all go back to wherever their ancestors came from, and give this land back to the Indians.

WAS THERE AN ETHIOPIAN IN THE WOODPILE?

The racists have, for years, fallen back on Genesis 9:25 (Noah's curse on Canaan) when trying to defend their treatment of Negroes. Why they think Canaan was black and the rest of the family was white has not been made clear. Possibly there was an Ethiopian in the woodpile! One of the best comments I have heard on this particular argument came from a colored minister, who told me that one of his parishioners had asked him why some of the white people put so much store by what a drunken sailor said to his son who had discovered him "naked," and paid so little attention to what God said.

For some reason or other, it is often the Bible-quoting segregationist who tries to convince you that his is the true faith, and that he is the one who really values his religion. Not silver nor gold can ever tempt him, he says, and he is without price, insofar as his virtue is concerned. But all too often these people who so earnestly sing, "Where He leads me, I will follow, I'll go with Him, with Him, all the way," say and do things that convince me they really wouldn't go more than half way, as they constantly ignore the second great commandment, in their treatment of Negroes.

These people always make me think of a story I read once in a nationally circulated magazine. When I make the application I am going to make, it isn't really funny at all, but is tragic. And stories such as these are the sort of thing most quickly condemned by the very people I am thinking about. But they will find something to criticize in what I say anyway, so I might as well give them something they can really get their teeth into. And their teeth and digestive tracts have shown amazing capabilities, as they repeatedly manage to strain at gnats and swallow camels (Matthew 23:23-24).

The story is about a socialite and her escort who were at a party, discussing women's virtue and the value placed on it. The gentleman had a theory, and to test it he asked the following question, "Would you spend the weekend with me, alone, at my country estate, for one million dollars?" The woman, after some hesitation, admitted that she probably would. Then came the next question, "Would you come up to my room with me later this evening for $5.00?" "Certainly not!" stormed the infuriated lady. "What do you think I am?" "We've established that," replied her escort, "now we are trying to determine your price."

I have been in discussion groups in which many of those present said that they valued their Christian faith above all else, that nothing would prevent them from living according to Christ's teachings, no matter what the cost.

If I had asked some of these people to stop disregarding several of Christ's teachings and try to give up their racial prejudice, they would have tried to change the subject, justify their actions by citing instances of prejudice in the North, or agree that racial prejudice is wrong but insist that changes have to come gradually. But in spite of all of the talk I'd know that they didn't plan to change a thing.

However, if I had suggested to these same people that they would be justified in taking a "social drink" in order to be popular, they would quickly let me know that they would never do this, as much as to say, "What do you think I am?"

So it seems that a good many people's devotion to their religious faith is much like the woman's virtue—a matter of price!

It is doubtful that many ministers really believe discrimination and segregation of Negroes is right, or that such practice would be advocated by Jesus Christ. If they did think it was right I'm sure they would preach on the subject nearly every week in order to enhance their popularity. But although they can't quite seem to stomach the idea of actively preaching *for* segregation, they rarely see fit to give encouragement to those who are ready and even anxious to give up their prejudice. Fear of offending church members, especially those who are heavy contributors, is the usual excuse given in private.

In the years since the tension over integrated schools in Little Rock, many people in the community have obviously lost much of their fervor for preserving racial segregation, and a good many give the impression that they would welcome many of the social changes that appear to be coming rapidly. And in spite of the fact that the Citizens Council groups

have repeatedly said that it is impossible to be a moderate
on the subject of integration, that one must either be for or
against, a lot of people obviously take a position somewhere
between racism and extreme liberalism. Many people in our
church have been enigmas to us, as we weren't sure just where
they stood. But their children often give them away. There
was a young woman who taught a Sunday school class, a good
friend of ours, who told my wife and me that in her class
of primary-aged children they frequently sang the well-known
words, "Jesus loves the little children, all the children of the
world, red or yellow, black or white, they are precious in His
sight." One Sunday, to give meaning to the words, the teacher
had cut out pictures of children of the different races mentioned. Each child in the class was asked to take one of the
pictures and pin it beneath the appropriate words of the song,
as they appeared on the blackboard. The child with the picture of a Negro refused to take her picture to the front, saying
that she wasn't going to put the picture of any "nigger" up
there. We were particularly saddened when we were told that
the little girl who refused was the child of one of the leaders
of our church.

I have listened to innumerable sermons by assorted preachers, in regular services or in revivals, for as many years as I
can remember. I cannot recall an instance where the one giving us our spiritual food did more than generalize about race
relations, although it seems to me that this is nothing more
or less than man's relationship to his fellow man. It is the
second most important thing we are taught in the Bible, right
behind love of God. But although the many preachers I have
listened to gladly got down to specifics, when they urged us to
refrain from various wrongdoings, and explained just why we
should not cheat on our income tax, gamble, neglect the
work of the church, and be guilty of the sin of indifference,
these men of the cloth were always painfully silent about the
sin of racial prejudice. In a lifetime of attending "revival

meetings" I have heard countless exhortations urging us to
bring *all* sinners into the fold, so that they might hear "the
Word." We were told that no sinner was so insignificant or
unattractive that he would not find a welcome in the house of
the Lord. I used to believe this, until recent years, when I
found that a person doesn't have to be insignificant or unattractive to find that he is unwelcome at a church. He can
accomplish it by merely being the wrong color. When it
comes to church membership there is no doubt that people
ordinarily join churches in their own neighborhoods and
usually join with people of their own economic background.
But when a man feels in need of spiritual guidance and there
is some particular minister he would like to hear, he should
be made to feel wanted in any congregation, regardless of his
color. A church is supposed to be the house of God, where
all who wish may come and worship. So it has been difficult
for me not to become cynical while listening to the "whosoever wills," knowing that there was always an unspoken exception. Many of us have realized, when listening to sermons
about loving our neighbors as we love ourselves, that there
was really an unspoken exception there, too. Of course, if the
subject of segregation had been mentioned, the segregationists
would have insisted that they really had more love for the
Negro than those of us who think Negroes have been despitefully used. Segregation, they would say, is best for the Negro
—most Negroes prefer it. But these segregationists have never
convinced me, and I doubt if they have convinced many
others, that they would relish or accept the things they say
the Negro is quite content with. The segregationist would say
that a Negro seeking entry to an all-white congregation was
not actually sincere, or that he would only be seeking to cause
trouble. But who is to say about this? Is it something to take
chances on? Our preachers would certainly say that it was not,
if the man in question were white. They would say they
wanted a chance to preach to the man, so that he might have

eternal life, as there might not be a second chance. I have often silently wondered if there might not be a good many segregationists in the church who would rather take the chance on the colored man's soul than to remove the barrier of segregation. But then, I should not judge. I hope that people will not feel this way.

Often, in times of crisis, I have waited hopefully, and always in vain, for at least a few words from the pulpit that might be of help to a people who were earnestly seeking the answers in times of racial tension. Such words rarely came, and when they did they were never direct or to the point. People hearing entreaties for brotherly love could always tell themselves that the preacher was really talking about the man in the office who was so cantankerous, or the next-door neighbor who was so disagreeable. Or perhaps he was referring to the heathen in Africa or South America. They were sure, they told themselves, that the preacher didn't mean that white children in public schools should speak a friendly word of greeting to some of the frightened Negro newcomers. They were sure, because he never, never put it this way. He just said that God was no respecter of persons. So the people in the congregation thought to themselves, Isn't it a shame the way people in Chicago treat visitors? Wasn't it terrible the things Hitler did to the Jews? How could people in some of the western states treat the Indians as they did, and still be good Christians? These must be the people the preacher was talking about. The preacher had certainly "hit the nail on the head"! Obviously, the people the preacher was thinking of didn't pay much attention to Christ's teachings, particularly to the Golden Rule. But although most of the people in the congregation managed to convince themselves that these were the things the preacher had in mind, they would just as soon he had chosen another subject, possibly subconsciously afraid the pastor would suddenly stop and point to them, and say, as Nathan said to David, "Thou art the man!" But the congregation needn't have worried. The preacher would have also known that he'd also have had accusing fingers pointing right back.

So we continued to get sermons admonishing us to give up the "things of the world," to abandon our selfish pleasures, to recognize our obligations to the Lord, to bring all our tithes into the storehouse so that, among other things, we can go to all peoples and preach the gospel, "even unto the uttermost parts of the world!"

I finally realized that we were never going to hear a good, straightforward sermon in more than a very small minority of Little Rock's churches, dealing more than superficially with the one major problem everyone was troubled about. Sometimes I began to have doubts, and wondered if Christ's message was something less than I had always believed. There were so many people I knew, good friends and acquaintances; I felt sure they were good Christians. Many certainly gave the appearance of working harder at their religion than I did. But they seemed to feel it entirely proper to exclude the Negro from all of their reckonings where so many of Christ's most important teachings and commandments were at stake. It all seemed very confusing and I finally decided that the only way to be fair would be to search the scriptures once again. I wished that we had done more of this type research prior to the writing of *This Is What We Found*. I found that it is impossible to turn more than a few pages anywhere in the New Testament without making the discovery that racial prejudice, unequal treatment because of race and the rejection of people because of their race is wrong, wrong, wrong! It seemed to me that if an average church member could see all of this, then preachers must have been trying desperately to avoid seeing the same thing, and trying even harder to avoid talking about it. I became convinced that most preachers know in their hearts segregation is wrong. "Be sure your sins will find you out" is a theme frequently expounded from our pulpits. It has been my observation that there is one sin not likely to be found out if the average preacher can help it.

As I sat through sermon after sermon, I began to wonder what kind of messages we might be hearing if there were just someone behind the pulpit not afraid to deliver them. I wondered what I would say, had I been blessed with the ability to preach and the opportunity. As I daydreamed through countless exhortations I mentally prepared a list of much needed sermons I could imagine myself delivering. As they are set down here they are not in sermon form. After all, I am a listener, not a preacher. But I think there is enough material in these short sermonettes so that any preacher worth his salt could build full-length sermons around them.

In some of the sermonettes you will notice frequent use of words in brackets, adjacent to well-known scripture verses. The words in brackets are the thoughts that have flashed through my mind as ministers have quoted these verses, always with some other application than the one I would make.

In my sermonettes, I thought I should concentrate on the New Testament and leave the Old Testament for my Jewish friends to interpret.

These friends often seem more inclined to follow some of Christ's important teachings than many Christians do.

LET MY PEOPLE GO

This is one sermon I'd preach with an Old Testament background, based on the story of the Jews in bondage, held captive in Egypt for four hundred years. To start my sermon I'd quote the first of the Ten Commandments, "Thou shalt have no other gods before me." I'd point out, as so many preachers have, that these gods or idols take many forms. They take the form of money, fame, success, and many other things. They might even take the form of race-caste. I'd ask my congregation if they did not believe it possible to make a god of racial segregation, and put this god ahead of the true God. I'd ask them, if they had to choose between these two, which god they would choose. Then I'd quote from Amos 9:7, where God tells the Jews, "Are ye not as the children of the Ethiopians unto me, O children of Israel?" And this would lead to another question for my congregation: If God equated the Jews, whom he classified as the chosen people, with Negroes, where does this leave the rest of us? In my Old Testament sermon, I'd not forget to point out that the Old Testament, as well as the New Testament, advocated friendliness, hospitality, and kindness to strangers, as indicated in Leviticus 19:34, "But the stranger that dwelleth with you shall be unto you . . . and thou shalt love him as thyself; for ye were strangers in the land of Egypt . . ."

And then I'd get to the main theme of my sermon, the story of four hundred years of Jewish slavery in Egypt. I'd not let my congregation forget that the "chosen people" were restricted to the dirtiest and most undesirable jobs to be had. I'd also point out that there were Jews who were not above selling out their leader Moses for their own personal gain, but that there had also been many Israelites who continued the struggle for freedom and retained their faith. Then I'd go on to say that there had been a people here, in the "land of the free," who had been kept in bondage of one sort or another for about four hundred years, and that it would seem four hundred years was long enough for any people to be slaves. In conclusion, I'd remind my congregation of the many Negroes who have never given up hope of full citizenship and freedom and who have retained their faith in God. I'd ask my congregation to ask themselves, as individuals, whether they would prefer to support someone like Moses, or someone like Pharaoh.

I would want to concentrate on New Testament sermons because so many times it is people who call themselves New Testament Christians who seem most anxious to "keep the nigger in his place." All of my New Testament sermons would have one basic theme; that there are two basic commandments, the first having to do with our love of God, and the second with love of our fellow man. Much of the New Testament is given over to the second great commandment. I'd have to tell my people that I found it difficult to turn more than a few pages, anywhere in the New Testament, without finding teachings which were applicable to problems having to do with racial prejudice. I'd tell them that there are hundreds of verses scattered throughout the New Testament which could and should be applied to the problems of prejudice, discrimination, and injustice, all of which are wrapped up in the segregation-integration controversy.

GO THOU AND DO LIKEWISE

The title of my second sermon would be, "Go Thou and Do Likewise." I'd quote, naturally, from the tenth chapter of Luke, which tells about the Good Samaritan. This is the story of a lawyer who asked Christ about eternal life. The lawyer told Christ that he had kept all of the commandments, even the one about loving his neighbor. With this Christ told of the man who had been waylaid by thieves, beaten, and left for dead, and how it was a member of a then-despised race who was the only person showing real concern and compassion. He took the injured man to a place he could be cared for and made arrangements to pay the injured man's bills. While all this had been going on, a prominent churchman, and a preacher, had passed by the injured man, "on the other side," and had ignored the injured man's needs. Christ then asked: "Which now of these three, thinkest thou, was the neighbour unto him that fell among the thieves?" And the lawyer said, "He that showed mercy on him." Christ then replied, "Go and do thou likewise."

It should not be necessary to add a great deal to this. I would point out that a man might be injured denying him the opportunity to get a skilled job for which he was qualified, the denial of dignity and the denial of many basic citizenship rights, and that the denials of these things could well be a greater injury than a beating or hunger.

A NEW COMMANDMENT I GIVE UNTO YOU

My next sermon would be on brotherhood. I would start by quoting from Romans 13:9–10: ". . . and if there be any other commandment, it is briefly comprehended in this saying, namely, Thou shalt love thy neighbour as thyself. Love worketh no ill to his neighbour: therefore love is the fulfilling of the law." And I'd read from John 13:34–35: "A new commandment I give unto you, That ye love one another . . . By this shall all men know that ye are my disciples, if you have love one to another." I'd preach to the white children in attendance, who were attending integrated schools and remind them that the colored children in their schools might be Christians, too, and hopeful of some evidence of Christian compassion from the white children. I'd encourage the white children to memorize Hebrews 13:2: "Be not forgetful to entertain strangers: for thereby some have entertained angels unawares." And I'd ask some of the more courageous children listening to convey a message to some of the frightened newcomers in their schools, a message from I John 3:13–15: "Marvel not, my brethren, if the world hate you. We know that we have passed from death unto life, because we love the brethren. He that loveth not his brother abideth in death.

Whosoever hateth his brother is a murderer: and ye know that no murderer hath eternal life abiding in him."

As I quoted these verses I'd tell of the words snarled at me in front of Central High: "You a 'nigger' lover?"

For those in my congregation who talked about love and compassion to others but were careful to withhold all but superficial love and compassion from Negroes, I'd quote from I John 3:17–18 and 23: "But whoso hath this world's good, and seeth his brother have need, and shutteth up his bowels of compassion from him, how dwelleth the love of God in him? My little children, let us not love in word, neither in tongue; but in deed and in truth . . . this is his commandment, That we should believe on the name of his Son Jesus Christ, and love one another, as he gave us commandment."

And for the parents who might be inclined to encourage their own children to make it as difficult for the Negro children in school as possible, I'd quote from I Peter 3:8–10: "Finally, be ye all of one mind, having compassion one of another; love as brethren, be pitiful, be courteous: Not rendering evil for evil, or railing for railing: but contrariwise blessing; knowing that ye are thereunto called, that ye should inherit a blessing."

In conclusion, in my sermon on brotherhood, I'd quote from I Peter 1:22–24: ". . . see that ye love one another with a pure heart fervently," and ". . . all flesh is as grass . . . The grass withereth, and the flower thereof falleth away."

I'd close by asking my listeners to practice brotherly love to all, including Negroes. And to those to whom a feeling of superiority seems of the utmost importance, I'd ask them to recall that "all flesh is grass."

STAND THOU THERE

My third sermon would be directed at those who have a feeling of superiority and who believe that they are entitled to preferential treatment in places of public accommodation. I would begin by telling of an experience I had soon after moving to Little Rock. As quite often happened, during those days, a discussion about Negroes arose at the coffee shop in my place of business. After hearing a particularly ardent segregationist expound at great length on why any white person was superior to any Negro, I finally felt called upon to say a word or two in defense of the Negro who was, as usual, not there to defend himself. The man who had spoken with such seeming authority gave me a pitying glance and asked contemptuously, "Do you think a nigger's as good as you are?"

"Which Negro?" I asked politely.

This seemed rather unexpected and an entirely new approach to my antagonist, but after some deliberation he shot back, "Any nigger."

"Well," I continued, "I'd have to know which Negro you are thinking about, and I'd have to know in which way you mean better. I'm sure there are Negroes who are better Christians than I. I'm positive there are Negroes who are better athletes. I found in college that some are smarter than I. Just what do you mean by 'better'?"

With this the man seemed to lose interest and walked out muttering to himself, shaking his head.

I'd tell this story instead of one of the standard Negro jokes so often told by pastors as introductions to their sermons, and then I'd read from James 2:2–10: "For if there come unto your assembly a man with a gold ring, in goodly apparel, and there came in also a poor man in vile raiment; And ye have respect to him that weareth the gay clothing, and say unto

him, Sit thou here in a good place; and say to the poor, Stand
thou there ["You'll have to move to the back of the bus,
nigger."], or sit here under my footstool: Are ye not then
partial in yourselves, and are become judges of evil thoughts?
Hearken, my beloved brethren, Hath not God chosen the
poor of this world rich in faith, and heirs of the kingdom
which he hath promised to them that love him? But ye have
despised the poor. Do not rich men oppress you, and draw
you before the judgment seats? Do not they blaspheme that
worthy name by the which ye are called? If ye fulfill the royal
law according to the Scripture, Thou shalt love thy neighbor
as thyself, ye do well: But if ye have respect to persons, ye
commit sin, and are convinced of the law as transgressors.
For whosoever shall keep the whole law, and yet offend in one
point, he is guilty of all."

I'd also call their attention to Romans 2:6–9 and 11, which
reads in part: "[God] will render to every man according to
hid deeds . . . Tribulation and anguish, upon every soul of
man that doeth evil; of the Jew first, and also the Gentile;
For there is no respect of persons with God." And I'd go on
to quote I Peter 1:17–18: "And if ye call on the Father, who
without respect of persons judgeth according to every man's
work, pass the time of your sojourning here in fear: Foras-
much as ye know that ye were not redeemed with corruptible
things, as silver and gold, from your vain conversation received by tradition from your fathers . . ." ["They've set our
race relations back one hundred years, these agitators upsetting our old traditions."]

I'd try to make my congregation see that although they
might previously have thought of the poor man in the story
as being white, he could easily have been, and no doubt more
likely would have been, colored. And it would then be easy
to ask if any members of the congregation had been guilty of
"respect of persons," or if it might not have been possible
that they had set themselves above God in this area by judg-

ing others according to their race or financial status, rather than "rendering every man according to his deeds." I'd ask the congregation what they, as individuals, would do if a colored person came to our church seeking to worship. Recently, when the new superintendent of schools moved into Little Rock, he was literally overwhelmed by calls and letters from churches asking that he give consideration to their church, as they said to him, "Sit thou here in a good place." But when three or four colored people sought entrance at one of Little Rock's downtown churches, they were told that they could go to the basement where there was a loudspeaker and they could listen to the sermon there. ("Sit here under my footstool.")

ARE WE BETTER THAN THEY?

My next sermon would be for the benefit of those who place such importance on alleged differences between races. I'd have to point out, of course, that Christ did not specifically mention how Negroes should be treated, any more than he mentioned treatment of Japanese, Mexicans, American Indians, or Anglo-Saxons. But he did use many examples of how racial, religious or nationality groups should be treated, using the oppressed minorities of his day as examples. I'd start out by reading from Acts 15:7–9: "And when there had been much disputing, Peter rose up, and said unto them, Men and brethren, ye know how that a good while ago God made choice among us, that the Gentiles by my mouth should hear the word of the gospel, and believe. And God, which knoweth the hearts, bare them witness, giving them the Holy Ghost, even as he did unto us; And put no difference between us and them, purifying their hearts by faith." Then, in Romans 3:9–10: "What then? are we better than they? No, in no wise: for we have before proved both Jews and Gentiles, that they are all under sin." And from Romans 10:12–13: "For there is no difference between the Jew and the Greek: for the same Lord over all is rich unto all that call upon him. For whosoever shall call upon the name of the Lord shall be saved." And Colossians 3:9–13: "Lie not one to another, seeing that ye have put off the old man with his deeds; And have put on the new man, which is renewed in knowledge after the image of him that created him: Where there is neither Greek nor Jew, circumcision nor uncircumcision, Barbarian, Scythian, bond nor free: but Christ is all, and in all. Put on therefore, as the elect of God, holy and beloved, bowels of mercies, kindness, humbleness of mind ["So you think a nigger's as good as you are?"], meekness, long-suffering; Forbearing one another, and forgiving one another, if any man have a quarrel against any: even as Christ forgave you, so also do ye."

In conclusion, I'd say that the complexities of racial differences should be left to the sociologists, physical differences to the medical profession, economic differences to the economists, but that as far as I could tell by reading the Bible, there are no differences that really matter and that although some might wish to substitute their judgment for God's, I'd personally be afraid to do so.

THE SOUNDING BRASS

My series of sermons would not be complete without a sermon on love, and I am speaking of the kind of love that might prompt someone to give a Negro a skilled job, providing he was qualified, even if by so doing the person making the job offer might jeopardize his own position. I am talking about a love that makes it possible to judge people according to the individual's ability, without taking race and color into consideration. There are many who, by making gifts of equal job opportunities, equal use of tax-supported facilities, and equal recognition of achievement, would be doing something that to them would be a real sacrifice. This would make these gifts of love even more meaningful to the giver.

My sermon on love would be found in Paul's First Epistle to the Corinthians, Chapter 13. I would ask my congregation to consider these verses and think of all the applications that could be made to life today, when silver-tongued orators make long and eloquent speeches in the halls of Congress, talking of states' rights, tradition, and custom, but with the real purpose of continuing withholding from 10 per cent of our population the kind of love we want to consider. I would ask my congregation to think carefully while the scripture verses were being read. The verses would be my sermon: "Though I speak with the tongues of men and of angels, and have not love, I am become as sounding brass, or a tinkling cymbal ["filibuster predicted"]. And though I have the gift of prophecy, and understand all mysteries, and all knowledge; and though I have all faith, so that I could remove mountains, and have not love, I am nothing. And though I bestow all my goods to feed the poor ["One thing about it, we've never let our niggers starve!"], and though I give my body to be burned, and have not love, it profiteth me nothing. Charity suffereth long, and is kind ["Why don't you kids give them nigger kids the silent treatment?"]; charity envieth not ["Look at that smart nigger in that Cadillac!"]; charity vaunteth not itself, is not puffed up ["And they expect us to eat with 'em!"], Doth not behave itself unseemly ["Two-four-six-eight, we don't wanna integrate"], seeketh not her own ["They got their own schools, ain't they?"], is not easily provoked, thinketh no evil ["Did you figure you needed to change yer luck?"]; rejoiceth not in iniquity [Nothing makes the racist happier than to read accounts of Negroes getting into trouble with the law], but rejoiceth in the truth ["We hold these truths to be self-evident: That all men are created equal;

that they are endowed by their Creator with certain unalienable rights . . ."]; Beareth all things, believeth all things, hopeth all things, endureth all things. Charity never faileth: but whether there be prophesies, they shall fail; whether there be tongues, they shall cease; whether there be knowledge, it shall vanish away. For we know in part, and we prophesy in part. But when that which is perfect is come, then that which is in part shall be done away. When I was a child, I spake as a child ["Did you hear the one about the ole nigger preacher?"], I understood as a child ["God wanted segregation, else why did he put races on different continents?"], I thought as a child ["You and me don't try to force ourselves into no country club"]: but when I became a man, I put away childish things. For now we see through a glass, darkly; but then face to face: now I know in part; but then I shall know even as also I am known ["Every man according to his deeds"]. And now abideth faith, hope, charity, these three; but the greatest of these is charity." Amen!

Now, I have quoted the King James version of the Bible which uses the word *charity*—a word often associated with welfare payments. But the primary meaning of this word is, of course, Christian love, and if you have any doubt on that score, look it up in a good dictionary.

YOUR RICHES ARE CORRUPTED

Many members of my congregation would no doubt think exploitation of human beings by other human beings an un-Christian act. But, here again an exception is usually made when Negroes are involved. There are many scripture verses that I have been told give a great deal of comfort to Negroes. I think it might be well for my congregation to hear them, beginning with James 5:1–6: "Go to now, ye rich men, weep and howl for your miseries that shall come upon you. Your riches are corrupted, and your garments are moth-eaten. Your gold and silver is cankered: and the rust of them shall be a witness against you, and shall eat your flesh as it were fire. Ye have heaped treasure together for the last days. Behold, the hire of the laborers who have reaped down your fields, *which is of you kept back by fraud,* crieth: and the cries of them which have reaped are entered into the ears of the Lord . . . Ye have lived in pleasure on the earth, and been wanton; ye have nourished your hearts, as in a day of slaughter. Ye have condemned and killed the just ["Yassuh, Mist' boss man"]; *and he doth not resist you."* (Italics mine.)

Whether or not there is something here needed by certain plantation owners I do not know. I suspect that there is. These scriptures might also apply to churches who pay Negro janitors a wage it would be impossible to keep a family on, and then complain because of the quality of the employee and about the marital status of the employee. I do know that Negroes have said these particular verses have been very helpful. They also enjoy reading from the Sermon on the Mount, Matthew 5:11–12: "Blessed are ye, when men shall revile you, and persecute you, and shall say all manner of evil against you falsely, for my sake. Rejoice, and be exceeding glad: for great is your reward in heaven: for so persecuted they the prophets which were before you." And from Luke 6:22, 27–28: "Blessed are ye when men shall hate you, *and when they shall separate you from their company* ["Nigger, go home!"], and shall reproach you, and cast out your name as evil ["You black ape!"], for the Son of man's sake . . . But I say unto you which hear, Love your enemies, do good to them which hate you, Bless them that curse you, and pray for them which despitefully use you." [kneel-in planned]. (Italics mine.)

WHENCE THEN HATH THIS MAN ALL THESE THINGS?

In my sermon on the trials and tribulation of Negroes I'd remind my listeners that often Negroes who have made good are denied recognition by the folks back home just because of their race. Thus, an all-American halfback from a Little Rock Negro high school had to go to the University of Michigan to achieve his all-American status. A halfback from Hot Springs had to go to the University of Illinois to display his talents and later be named outstanding player in the annual college all-star football game.

These and many other Negro sports stars have grown up in many parts of the South, but the segregationists back home seldom think of them as home-town boys. To them these great athletes are just "smart niggers" who didn't know their place. It is good to know that there are many others in the South who feel differently, as was displayed in the welcome given to Wilma Rudolph, outstanding woman Olympic athlete, when she returned to Clarksville, Tennessee. For those who feel badly because they are denied the recognition they feel they have earned, they get consolation by remembering that it was always so, even in Jesus' day, as related in Matthew 13:55–58: "Is not this the carpenter's son? is not his mother called Mary? and his brethren, James, and Joses, and Simon, and Judas? And his sisters, are they not all with us? Whence then hath this man all these things? And they were offended in him. But Jesus said unto them, A prophet is not without honor, save in his own country. . . ."

I'd tell my congregation about sitting through a closed-circuit TV movie showing a championship boxing match. One of the contenders was from another land. He was known to be quite a playboy and had been blessed with much of this

world's good. The other man was an American—a product
of an orphan home, and of a home for emotionally disturbed
children. He was shy and rather afraid of people. Normally,
under such circumstances, it would have been natural for the
people in the theater to cheer their fellow American, since he
had battled all sorts of odds to get where he was. But
strangely, when the American had scored a surprise victory
over the champion, he was loudly booed by many of the people in the audience. The American, you see, was black.

And I'd continue by telling of the three representatives
from the country of Nigeria who visited in Little Rock. They
stayed in one of the best hotels, ate freely in any restaurant,
and were invited to speak in one of the larger churches in
the city, and in general were given the red-carpet treatment as
they walked about in their native costumes; but these black
people, you see, were not Americans.

So I would conclude by saying that in view of their history,
it is no wonder that so many colored people take much comfort in the knowledge that history is filled with accounts of
people who have risen above the stigma of coming from a
certain town, a certain country, or a certain race. And they
know that even Christ had the same problem, as he heard it
said, "Can any good thing come out of Nazareth?"

HE SHALL CHANGE THE CUSTOMS

A sermon would be needed for those bound by tradition.
Many of these people would have you believe also that segregation, if it is a tradition, is *the* southern tradition. I find
many worthwhile traditions in the southern heritage, but legal
segregation of Negroes has only been in effect in the South
for about sixty years. So it could hardly be called an "old"
tradition. And considering the many worthwhile traditions,
the idea that keeping the "nigger" in his place is the primary

southern tradition is an insult to the many southerners who
concentrate on the traditions of courtesy, friendliness, honor,
and truth.

In my sermon I would naturally remind my congregation
that few have displayed as little concern for tradition as Jesus
Christ. He defied tradition any time he thought tradition
wrong. There were several examples, starting with the story
found in Luke 15:1-4: "Then drew near unto him all the
publicans and sinners for to hear him. And the Pharisees and
scribes murmured, saying, This man receiveth sinners, *and
eateth with them.* And he spake this parable unto them, saying, What man of you, having a hundred sheep, if he lose one
of them, doth not leave the ninety and nine in the wilder-
ness, and go after that which is lost, until he find it?" (Again,
italics mine.) After telling this story I'd ask my people if
they think Jesus would refuse to have Negroes in his home,
or refuse to share a lunch counter with them or advocate
denying them entrances at places of public accommodation
because of their race. I'd ask members of my congregation if
they would expect Christ to turn a Negro away from a church
door, or if they did not think it more likely he would welcome
the Negro, the same as he would any man, thinking that by
so doing the one hundredth man might be returning to the
fold.

I'd tell about Jesus' passage through Jericho, and his invitation to the house of Zaccheus, who belonged to a group that
was thoroughly disliked, a group with which most people
refused to associate. And I'd quote from Luke 19:7: "And
when they saw it, they all murmured, saying, That he was
gone to be guest with a man that is a sinner." And John 4:9
would also have a message for those fearful of breaking tradition. This was when Jesus stopped and talked to a Samaritan
woman and asked that she draw him a drink of water. She
said, "How is it that thou, being a Jew, askest drink of me,
which am a woman of Samaria? for the Jews have no dealings

with the Samaritans." Later, as the disciples came upon them, it was said that the disciples marveled that he talked with the woman; "yet no man said, What seekest thou? or, Why talkest thou with her?" (John 4:27).

And Jesus continued to break traditions which he felt needed to be broken. We read in John 5:9–16: "And immediately the man was made whole, and took up his bed, and walked: and on the same day was the sabbath. The Jews therefore said unto him that was cured, It is the sabbath day: it is not lawful for thee to carry thy bed . . . Afterward Jesus findeth him in the temple, and said unto him, Behold, thou art made whole: sin no more, lest a worse thing come unto thee. The man departed, and told the Jews that it was Jesus, which had made him whole. And therefore did the Jews persecute Jesus, and sought to slay him . . ."

Christ's disciples, too, got in trouble because of their disregard for tradition. The martyred Stephen had to contend with these close adherents of tradition, as explained in Acts 6:14: "For we have heard him say, that this Jesus of Nazareth shall destroy this place, and shall change the customs which Moses delivered us."

In the conclusion of my sermon on breaking tradition I'd point out that the reason that the political and religious leaders of Jesus' day persecuted him and permitted his crucifixion was that they had a good thing going and would stop at nothing to prevent Christ from speaking the truth.

HAVE WE NOT PROPHESIED IN THY NAME?

Of course, I'd want to preach a sermon on humility and direct it primarily at those who have an inflated opinion of their own importance because of being born into a privileged group. These are the people who so often mistake vanity for "race pride." I guess I'd start off by reading from Matthew

7:1–5: "Judge not, that ye be not judged . . . and with what measure ye mete, it shall be measured to you again. And why beholdest thou the mote that is in thy brother's eye, but considerest not the beam that is in thine own eye? Or how wilt thou say to thy brother, Let me pull out the mote out of thine eye; and, behold, a beam is in thine own eye? Thou hypocrite, first cast out the beam out of thine own eye . . ." After reading these verses I'd ask how many had engaged in the popular pastime of making fun of the morals of Negroes, including Negro pastors and church leaders. I'd go on to say that immorality in any form should not be encouraged or condoned, but I'd remind them of the many white men who have, from a position of great advantage, willingly contributed to the immorality of Negro women, who have usually been in a position of great disadvantage. I'd point out that immorality among white people is often covered up by means not always available to Negroes. And I'd say to all, "Let him who is without sin among you, cast the first stone."

To church workers who are inclined toward much loud praying in public, even though it seems obvious they want to make exceptions of Negroes in the application of many Christian principles, I'd read from Matthew 7:21–23: "Not every one that saith unto me, Lord, Lord, shall enter into the kingdom of heaven; but he that doeth the will of my Father which is in heaven. Many will say to me in that day, Lord, Lord, have we not prophesied in thy name? and in thy name have cast out devils? and in thy name done many wonderful works? And then will I profess unto them, I never knew you: depart from me, ye that work iniquity." I would then go on to tell my congregation that they might well be in daily violation of Christ's second great commandment, as they showed only superficial love for their colored neighbors instead of showing real love by granting human dignity, offering equal job opportunities and equal justice under the law.

For those who laugh at the humility of the Negro and at

the same time consider themselves quite superior, I would
recommend the reading of I Peter 5:5–6 (italics mine):
"Likewise, ye younger, submit yourselves unto the elder. Yea,
all of you be subject one to another, and be clothed with
humility: *for God resisteth the proud, and giveth grace to
the humble.* Humble yourselves therefore under the mighty
hand of God, that he may exalt you in due time." And I'd
go on to tell my listeners about the Negro parent who had
told me of the assurance he felt that God had given grace to
the humble, to his child, as he was given strength to face the
terrors he expected in the newly integrated school.

I'd point out to my congregation that it is not uncom-
mon for some of them to call Negro men "boy," even though
the men may be fifty years old. Then I would read from Matthew 18:4–6: "Whosoever therefore shall humble himself as
this little child, the same is greatest in the kingdom of
heaven. And whoso shall receive one such little child in my
name receiveth me. But whoso shall offend one of these little
ones which believe in me, it were better for him that a millstone were hanged about his neck, and that he were drowned
in the depth of the sea." And then I would ask my congregation if it just might not be possible for some of the "little
ones" to be represented by colored students in newly integrated schools, who were counting on the Christian training
of some of the white students to help them get through the
difficult transition period, or, the little ones might be white
students who were trying to do the right thing, and follow
Christ's teachings in their race relations, but looked in vain
for Christian guidance from many of their elders.

NOT AS OTHER MEN ARE

A sermon on hypocrisy would be a must. Segregationists have often attempted to justify the restrictions placed on Negroes on the grounds that many of the people advocating equal rights and justice were actually being hypocritical, because they, while advocating peaceful school integration, did not practice integration in their churches. While such accusations serve no useful purpose, other than to confuse the issue, there have probably been many times when the accusations were justified. But two wrongs do not make a right, and I would get into my sermon by quoting from Titus 1:15–16: "Unto the pure all things are pure: but unto them that are defiled and unbelieving is nothing pure; but even their mind and conscience is defiled. They profess that they know God; but in works they deny him, being abominable, and disobedient, and unto every good work reprobate." And further, from Matthew 23:23–28: "Woe unto you, scribes and Pharisees, hypocrites! for ye pay tithe of mint and anise, and cummin, and have omitted the weightier matters of the law, judgment, mercy, and faith: these ought ye to have done, and not to leave the other undone. Ye blind guides, which strain at a gnat [card playing, dancing, movies, smoking, minor doctrinal matters], and swallow a camel [violations of the second great commandment, the Golden Rule and the "royal law"]. Woe unto you, scribes and Pharisees, hypocrites! for ye make clean the outside of the cup and of the platter, but within they are full of extortion and excess. Thou blind Pharisee, cleanse first that which is within the cup and platter, that the outside of them may be clean also. Woe unto you, scribes and Pharisees, hypocrites! for ye are like unto whited sepulchres, which indeed appear beautiful outward, but are within full of dead men's bones, and of all uncleanness."

These are strong words, and I would ask my congregation if some of the words might not apply to them, who "do all good works." They pay their tithe, they teach Sunday school classes, they rise to testify, they walk the aisles periodically for rededication, but would never consider giving up their prejudice for their Lord. They attempt to justify their violation of Christ's teachings about human relations by all manner of artifice.

Then I'd go on to the first three verses in John 16: "These things have I spoken unto you, that ye should not be offended. They shall put you out of the synagogues ["We don't want any disturbance."]: yea, the time cometh, that whosoever killeth you will think that he doeth God service [The man arrested for master-minding bombing of the Little Rock school-board building had just come from prayer meeting in a segregationist church!]. And these things will they do unto you, because they have not known the Father, nor me."

Most important, I'd get into regional bickering over which part of America, North or South, really treats the Negro best. This is really a case of the pot calling the kettle black, and you can take your choice as to which is which. What Americans both North and South seem to forget is that as far as their treatment of minority groups is concerned, they are both a great deal like the man mentioned in Luke 18:11–14: "The Pharisee stood and prayed thus with himself, God, I thank thee, that I am not as other men are, extortioners ["It's a crime the way those plantation owners exploit those poor Negroes"], unjust ["I notice the niggers push brooms up North, too"], adulterers ["They just don't have any morals"], or even as this publican. I fast twice in the week ["The white people pay 99 per cent of the taxes"], I give tithes of all that I possess ["Here's five dollars for the Urban League"]. And the publican, standing afar off, would not lift up so much as his eyes unto heaven ["I know that I'm prejudiced, but I'm honestly trying to overcome it"], but smote upon his breast, saying, God be merciful to me a sinner. I tell you, this man went down to his house justified rather than the other: for every one that exalteth himself ["What have they ever done, without the help of the white man?"] shall be abased; and he that humbleth himself shall be exalted."

I'd conclude this sermon with a plea for all of us, North or South, to make a real effort to obey Christ's second great commandment, wherever we happen to live.

RENDER UNTO CAESAR

At least one sermon should be preached on loyalty to and respect for the government of the United States of America. This becomes increasingly clear when we read about state officials using phrases such as "Kennedy's Koon Klan," and "stupid little brother Bobby." Such talk certainly does nothing to stem the tide or to change anyone's mind about segregation, one way or the other. But it certainly "types" the people who have nothing better to offer in the way of resistance to change.

The text for this sermon would be found in Luke 20:20–25: "And they watched him, and sent forth spies [State Sovereignty Commission], which should feign themselves just men, that they might take hold of his words, that so they might deliver him unto the power and authority of the governor ["I will stand in the schoolhouse door!"]. And they asked him, saying, Master, we know that thou sayest and teachest rightly, neither acceptest thou the person of any, but teachest the way of God truly: Is it lawful for us to give tribute unto Caesar, or no? But he perceived their craftiness, and said unto them, Why tempt ye me? Show me a penny. Whose image and superscription hath it? They answered and said, Caesar's. And he said unto them, Render therefore unto

Caesar the things which be Caesar's, and unto God the things which be God's."

With this I'd certainly have to tell my congregation that there have been countless times in recent years when much tension and trouble could have been avoided had the people of America, particularly those obsessed with the idea of retaining race-caste, remembered these words of Christ.

A case in point, although there have been many others, is the tragedy that occurred at the University of Mississippi in the fall of 1962. The events that transpired there may have crystallized a good many people's ideas about the real by-products of racial segregation. We had heard many times and been told many times about the "real" love and compassion that many strong segregationists have had for Negroes, and it is true that there have been countless instances of kindness, at the personal level. But we see all of this in true perspective when hundreds of college students shout obscenities at a lone Negro, and sing, "We will bury all Negroes, in the Mississippi mud." It then becomes clear that the love they talk about lasts only as long as the Negro voluntarily remains in the Mississippi mud and gives the impression that he is happy to be there. But when he tries to lift himself out of it, all hell breaks loose.

Probably no people have been more outspoken than the people of Mississippi about what they term federal interference. This, of course, does not apply in certain areas, since in 1962 Mississippi got back four dollars in federal grants of one kind or another for every dollar they paid to the federal government. Still, they try to convince you that the government of the United States of America is the enemy of its people. Surely, nothing could be farther from the truth. If Christ expected the people of his day to have respect for and abide by the laws of a government which enslaved its subjects, how much more would he expect people to respect a government which has made men free?

HE IS GUILTY OF ALL

My last sermon would be, basically, a résumé of all the others. Its central theme would be the Golden Rule. The Golden Rule is quite simple, and easy to understand. It is this simplicity, I suppose, that so infuriates the racist whenever this guide for living is mentioned in connection with Negroes. The segregationist can talk his way around many of the usual pleas for tolerance and brotherly love which are found throughout the New Testament. They invariably fall back on the theory that their way is best for the Negro, and that the Negro prefers to be segregated from the mainstream of American life. But they cannot talk fast enough to fit their theories into the Golden Rule, nor can they fit the Golden Rule into their theories. I think it is probably pretty clear that the last thing most of those advocating segregation would want is to be treated as Negroes have been treated in America for so many years. So for the most part the segregationists avoid the discussion of this particular teaching of Jesus—at least insofar as it would apply to race relations. I would remind my congregation that they have no more right to ignore this truth than they do any of the rest of Christ's teachings.

Knowing that many of my congregation would be quick to tell me that they had never "mistreated" a Negro, I'd want to explore the subject of just what constitutes mistreatment. I'd have to say to all, "Would you want to be denied a decent, skilled job you were entirely capable of handling, just because of your race? Would you like it if people kept writing letters to the editor of your daily newspaper, and some of these letters were so vile and vicious toward all members of your race that they bordered on libel? Would you like it when politicians condemn all members of your race even though you as an individual and as a Christian were guilty of none of the things mentioned? Would you think it fair after spending money in department stores to be denied a cup of coffee and a sandwich at the lunch counter of that same store, just because of your race? Would you like it if, after having sacrificed and put yourself through college, and then gone on to achieve success, you were either ridiculed or ignored, just because of your race? Would you think it right if you were denied entrance to hotels, restaurants, parks, and other places of public accommodations? Would you like to be attacked by hoodlums because of insisting on non-discriminatory treatment on buses, which you had been told was your constitutional right by your government? Would you like to be cursed, spat at, threatened, or simply ignored because you enrolled at an integrated school in line with the stated policy of your government? In short, would you want to be denied most of the basic rights and privileges of citizenship that all other Americans take for granted—the things that your history teachers, preachers, and politicians have told you all your lives that you had a right to expect? If you think you would like to be denied all these things because of something you had nothing to do with, and regardless of how you as an individual conduct yourself, then go ahead and do these things to Negroes, or support a system that does it to Negroes. But if you don't think you would like it, and if you think you would feel it unfair if you were on the receiving end of it; if you consider yourselves Christian and want to be effective disciples of the Christ you profess to follow, then *stop making an exception of the Negro!* In the real application of so many of Christ's teachings, remember that "Whosoever shall keep the whole law, and yet offend in one point, he is guilty of all."

These are the sermons I think should be preached. I haven't heard them preached, except occasionally on television by Billy Graham, and I doubt if sermons like them will be heard, at least for another ten or fifteen years. By then the church may have caught up with the law, the sports world, the entertainment world, the Jewish organizations, the educators, the government, and the youth of America, in placing Christian principles into effect where race is a factor. Then they will no doubt tell us from the pulpits, "Why, this is what we have been preaching all along!"

Chapter 8

SERMONS I'D BORROW

The sermons in the previous chapter were the products of my own imagination (with a big assist from the Bible, of course). There are two "borrowed" sermons I wish everyone could hear. They came to me in pamphlet form and have been read by a good many racial liberals. I wish they could be read, or listened to, by many more.

The first is by Ross Coggins, a highly regarded Southern Baptist, a former missionary now associated with the Southern Baptist Convention's Christian Life Commission.

In the foyer of our church, as is the case in many churches, there are generally available various religious tracts and pamphlets for any who might wish to pick them up and read them.

The following borrowed sermon, "Missions and Race,"[1] was published by the Christian Life Commission, and was made available to convention churches, but for some reason or other, none of these pamphlets ever found their way into our foyer. I suspect this was probably true of most other churches which received sample copies.

[1] "Missions and Race" first appeared in *Christianity Today* (January 17, 1964, issue); Copyright © 1964 by Christianity Today, Inc., and is reprinted with permission of Christianity Today, Inc.

"MISSIONS AND RACE"[1]

Today's missionary navigates his faith in strange waters, crowded with other craft. It taxes all his powers to contend with the swift currents of nationalism, superstition, Communist subversion, and resurgent indigenous religion. He requires—and profoundly deserves—the total support of his homeland constituency.

Missionaries are painfully aware of their vulnerability in these changing times. Perhaps the most damaging area of this vulnerability is at the point of race relations. That Christians in America would tolerate, even justify, the enormities of racism is an enigma which is at once the dismay of the missionary and the delight of his adversaries. Race prejudice today is a liability we cannot afford. It perverts our gospel, challenges our sincerity, dissipates our witness, and "gives great occasion for the enemies of God to blaspheme" (II Samuel 12:14).

The Missionary's Personal Struggle With Race Prejudice

At the risk of disillusioning you, let me begin by stating that race prejudice is, first of all, the missionary's personal problem. This may offend the widespread angelic fallacy we cherish toward all foreign missionaries, but it is a note of realism clearly indicated. It is altogether possible for a Christian to arrive on foreign shores and discover that any effective ministry must be deferred until he solves his own race problem. Contingent upon the solution of this problem is an entire lifetime of usefulness.

Every missionary realizes that true camaraderie with na-

[1] "Missions and Race" first appeared in *Christianity Today* (January 17, 1964, issue); Copyright © 1964 by Christianity Today, Inc., and is reprinted with permission of Christianity Today, Inc.

tionals is slow to congeal, quick to melt. The faintest hint of race prejudice in a missionary's attitude cannot be concealed from nationals; it is almost as if they can smell it. It is regrettable in the extreme when any missionary gives the impression, "The Lord has led me out here to help you people; kindly keep out of my way while I do it." Latent prejudice is exposed by an imperious tone, by the tendency to pauperize nationals through a readiness to give and a reluctance to receive in return, by obvious resentment at working under national supervision, by the habitual choice of white people for social companionship, by disregarding the opinions of nationals, and particularly by the God-is-an-American-and-his-skin-is-white-like-mine attitude. This last confuses Christianizing with Americanizing, superimposing programs upon people which have about as much relevance to their culture as bird tracks on the moon. Far too often, missionaries have tenaciously resisted any adaptation of the gospel to indigenous cultural patterns.

The very name "missionary" is a handicap in some parts of the world where it has been associated with the superior-inferior relationships of colonial days. The so-called "Great White Father" image of the missionary is dangerously anachronistic in modern times. Happy is that missionary who can walk among his people as an equal and a brother, maintaining a careful distinction between his timeless gospel and his Western cultural trappings.

A Hindering Heritage

Despite its origin in the Middle East, Christianity is universally regarded as a Western religion. Until fairly recent times, mission work was done largely in lands under colonial rule. As a result, missionaries inevitably came to be identified with a system under which the control of "natives" was deemed "the white man's burden." As T. S. Eliot has stated so well, "Of all that was done in the past, you eat the fruit, either rotten or ripe . . . for every ill deed in the past we suffer the consequence."[2] Colonial governments, usually so-called Christian countries, sometimes incurred such hatred as can only be understood as a reaction to the indignities of race prejudice, not just bitterness over economic exploitation. "No Indonesians or Dogs Allowed," said the sign in a Dutch restaurant in Djakarta in earlier days. Christian missionaries could not avoid being associated with the general aura of white paternalism and superiority. This explains why some national leaders consider Christian missions as vestigial colonialism, an intolerable reminder of the past.

Since World War II a universal declaration of independence has taken place which has seen forty-three new nations emerge. These young nations are often unable to cope with their problems because the colonial governments did not consider them worthy of educational preparation (with notable exceptions). For instance, when 13 million Congolese were freed by the Belgians, there were only sixteen college graduates among them. In 1940, Indonesia had only one hundred and fifty-seven students in colleges and universities, out of a population of over seventy million.

Is it difficult to understand the distrust of these people toward all white men, the missionaries included? "Christianity is the religion of the white man," said a Muslim leader in Indonesia, "Shun it."

Soon after we arrived in Indonesia we noticed our household helpers customarily knelt when they served us refreshments. It seemed a degrading and unnecessary thing, and we discontinued it against the advice of our Dutch neighbor. "They enjoy it," he confided. On one occasion this same

[2] T. S. Eliot. Choruses from "The Rock." *The Complete Poems and Plays:* 1909–1950. New York: Harcourt Brace and Co., 1952.

neighbor overheard me address the Indonesian postman as
Tuan, the Indonesian equivalent of Mister. "You simply *must*
not treat these people as equals," he insisted. We felt, however, that the Christian thing to do was always to *Tuan* to
others as we would have them *Tuan* to us. If that is poor
humor, it is good religion. It is only through dissociating himself from the embarrassing heritage of colonialism that the
modern missionary can gain an entrance into the hearts of
people.

The Effect of American Racial Tension on World Missions

One of the most appalling stigmata of our time is the great
gulf fixed between our gospel and our conduct in the eyes of
the world. Early missionaries could observe a discreet silence
about race prejudice in their homelands, but this is impossible in today's world. We cannot hide the abysmal disparity
between our preachment and our practice.

> In times of swift communication,
> Nation cannot hide from nation
> What it does. Within brief hours
> Headlines shout how hatred's powers
> Close love's doors with jarring thud
> Because of race, because of blood.

Racial tension in your home town exerts a seismic effect on
world missions. Our missionaries around the world describe
our racial discrimination as a veritable millstone around the
neck of Christian missions.

Consider some questions your missionaries are compelled
to answer every day. Why are churches in America segregated? How can Christianity and racial discrimination be
reconciled? Why am I refused admittance into a Baptist
school in America when I am welcome in a Russian university? How can you explain German bestiality during the

war in the light of their Christian heritage? And perhaps the worst question of all: Why do you believe Christianity will do so much more for my country than it has for yours?

There are some answers to questions like these, but they sound very hollow half-a-world away from home. The fact is, we have permitted the gog-magogery of our race failures to neutralize the effectiveness of our missionaries. They are at the forefront of our struggle against the powers of evil, and we have weakened their hands. On mission fields this struggle has Darwinian overtones, for only the fittest can survive. Will we continue to supply weapons for the enemy's hands?

On the day after the Russians orbited their first astronaut, I happened to be in the airlines office in Bandung. Standing just behind me at the counter was a tall Russian who was in Bandung to attend an Asia-Africa conference of some kind. The lobby was crowded with delegates from the various countries, each of whom embraced the Russian and congratulated him upon the splendid achievement in outer space. I was frankly jealous for my own country.

The Russian and I fell into a lengthy conversation which was frequently interrupted by these jovial salutations from passing delegates. I, too, congratulated the Russian and then asked him about the conference. "The most satisfying reports," he said, "have come from the new nations in Africa. These people at last are throwing off the shackles of colonialism and imperialism."

I replied that my own country warmly approved every step forward these people were taking, and expressed disappointment that an American voice could not declare this to the conference.

"They would not listen," declared the Russian. "They would feel you had no right to speak."

I knew what he was getting at, but I had a morbid desire to hear him say it. I asked him to explain.

He replied with ill-concealed satisfaction, "Many of these African delegates have been to your country. They have met your Mr. Jim Crow—I believe that is his name." Then he tapped me on the chest with his forefinger and concluded, "This Jim Crow is your delegate to our conference. He is your number one ambassador to these people."

In a day when Marxists are calling every man *comrade*, let us not refuse to call any man *brother*.

A Time for Action

It is difficult to say anything on the race problem which is not repetitious or platitudinous. Our dilemma does not stem, however, from lack of words but from lack of action. It is astounding how often and how well this issue is addressed. The time has come and now is for Christian action to turn the oughts to shalls.

There is no denying that our continued toleration of an oppressive status quo stems from a timorous disinclination to translate into action the New Testament revelation of God's love.

What does it mean that all men are equally the objects of God's love? It means that all the ways we separate or humiliate others are an offence to God. It means that every child has the right to grow up with a sense of dignity and worth. It means that no man must live out his days indentured to "his place." It means that all our stratagems of evasion are intolerable in the sight of God.

More specifically, the love of God means that we should treat every man as a human being. We should throw open our hospital doors to any man seeking healing. We should open our educational institutions to any man seeking knowledge. There should be no racially imposed barriers to equal citizenship, employment opportunity, or access to public recreation facilities. Above all, let every church abide by the sign placed in front of so many churches: EVERYBODY WELCOME. Paul expressed this concept with eloquent simplicity when he wrote to Philemon concerning the runaway slave, Onesimus: "Receive him . . . as a brother" (Philemon 15, 16).

I am not suggesting that we should lightly cast aside our Southern traditions; I am suggesting that we throw them aside with great force wherever they violate the spirit and teaching of the New Testament. We must obey God rather than men.

This, of course, can be quite costly. The son of one of our Southern Baptist missionaries participated in the "kneel-ins" in New Orleans churches. Writing about his motivation, he stated:

My philosophy in regard to the "kneel-ins" is complex and at several points even contradictory. First of all, I should explain that my parents are Southern Baptist missionaries. My father went to the Southern Baptist Seminary. Consequently I grew up without any prejudice of the racial variety and with the strong belief that the church was the Church of Christ, not of men. Since then I have seriously doubted that belief. I detest any form of bigotry and discrimination, despite the fact that I have lived in the South for six years. Although I understand completely the reasons and mores behind segregation I have never been able to rationalize them with my Christian principles. I have come to "tolerate" segregated public facilities but have never been able to say "white church" without feeling deep sorrow and pain. This is the underlying belief which has led me to decide to do something positive in an attempt to eliminate discrimination, even at the risk of personal loss of liberty. . . . You must realize that because of my belief I have spent two days in jail and am facing the possibility of ten years of hard labor. The state of Louisiana has charged me with "criminal anarchy" and will prosecute this charge early next month. If a man is not willing to suffer for his convictions, they are not worth the trouble having. (Quoted from a letter October 1, 1960.)

If we are unwilling to pay this kind of price for our convictions, we can at least try to lead our churches to a realistic understanding of our world mission. What profound dichotomy has enabled Southern Baptists to believe in world missions abroad and racial discrimination at home? Many of our failures obviously stem from a lack of information about the relation of racism to missionary outreach. Race prejudice and foreign missions are mutually exclusive, for missions simply means sharing the gospel with the races; it is the gospel in world perspective.

Missionaries believe they have a right to expect this note to be sounded with courage from pulpits here in America. Needless to say, they are often bitterly disappointed. Their courage in going to the ends of the earth is often unmatched by Christian leaders at home who blandly ignore the existence of a problem. In the chaotic world of today, can the bland lead the bland?

Our five-year-old daughter was born and spent her early life in Indonesia. She learned Indonesian before she spoke English, and she was very devoted to her little Indonesian friends and playmates. Her orientation was far more Indonesian than we realized at the time. When we returned to the United States she was quite intimidated by her new surroundings. She tended to identify with Negroes when she saw them, often addressing them in Indonesian. In her insecurity she clung to her mother or to me and constantly inquired about when we'd be going back to Indonesia. We tried to surround her with all the patience and love she so obviously needed. I don't know just when she began to come around. Perhaps it was when she was really received into the pre-school gang on our street, or when we got her a kitten, or made a snowman. One day she sat on my lap, looked up and said, "Daddy, I belong here, don't I!" Life has taken on rich new meaning since then.

May God help us to create the kind of a world in which every man can lift up his head and say, "I belong here."

"THIS I BELIEVE"

This is the second of my borrowed sermons. It was given before an adult church school class at Trinity Presbyterian Church, Atlanta, Georgia, on January 1, 1961. Dr. Haywood N. Hill was teacher of the class and an elder in the church. Dr. Hill's address has been widely distributed in pamphlet form and has been read by many. I hope that its appearance here makes it possible for it to be read by many, many more. Dr. Hill said:

I am a Southerner. I was bred in the South where my forefathers were slave holders and Confederate soldiers. I was born and raised in Southern towns with their rigid racial patterns and their typical Southern prejudice. I was away from the South for a few years, but returned to live in the South by choice and intend to remain here for the rest of my life. I love the South and its people.

I like to have two black arms in my kitchen and two black legs pushing my lawn mower, to help take the drudgery out of living for myself and my family, and I like having them at a very minimum cost to me.

I like choosing my own friends and associates, and I like

eating in pleasant places with well-bred people of my own
race, class and status.

I like to worship in a church which is composed of my
friends and equals where I will be among my own group,
racially, socially and intellectually.

I like for my children to go to school with their own kind
and with other children of their own social, racial and intel-
lectual level. I like for them to be shielded from poverty,
ignorance, dirt and disease.

I like to practice medicine among intelligent, cooperative
people who understand what I am trying to do for them,
who are friends as well as patients, and who pay their bills.

I like to live in a neighborhood composed of people of
my own group who have pleasant, well-kept homes, and
where there is no strife or conflict.

I do not want my daughter to marry a Negro.

I like the racial status quo. I am a Southerner.

But, I am also a Christian. As a Christian I must believe
that God created all men and that all men are equal in the
sight of God. I must believe that all men are my brothers
and are children of God, and that I am my brother's keeper.
I must believe that Jesus meant what he said when he commanded me to love my neighbor as myself, and when he
commanded me to do unto others as I would have them do
unto me. I must believe that the church is God's house and
that it does not belong to me, to the congregation of Trinity Presbyterian Church, or to the Southern Presbyterian
Church. I must believe in the fellowship of all believers.

I am also a scientist and have devoted my life to the pur-
suits of objective truth. Therefore, I must know that while
there are individual differences among people that there is no
such thing as racial inferiority. I must know that within every
group there are individuals with different potentialities, and
that I cannot arbitrarily classify anyone on the basis of his
race or color. I must know that poverty and ignorance and

isolation, call it segregation if you will, breed feelings of inferiority, frustration, resentment, and despair and that these
feelings in turn lead to misery, to immorality, and to crime
which, in turn, not only depress the people and the communities involved but the community as a whole and the
whole country.

Therefore, as a Christian and as a scientist I am obligated
to act on the basis of what I know and what I believe and not
on the basis of what I like. I must live by conviction and by
conscience rather than by preference and by prejudice.

I must, therefore, regard every man, rich or poor, black
or white, as a child of God and as a person, not as some kind
of sub-human being or animal or even as an inferior. I must
try to see to it that every individual gets equal rights under
the law and in politics. This applies particularly to the right
of equal justice in the courts and the right to exercise political
privilege; that is, the right to vote. If I fear the effects of bloc
voting and voting from ignorance, then I must see to it that
every man is educated to the point where he votes intelli-
gently.

I am obligated to pay a living wage to every man who
works for me and to do my best to see that others do the
same. I must accord to every man the right to rise to the limit
of his abilities in any job or profession, and I must make
every attempt to see that no man is blocked because of his
race or his social status. If any individual of any race rises to
a position equal to mine, then I must accord to him the
same privileges that I have and welcome him as an equal.

I must see to it that everyone has an opportunity for an
education as good as my own children have. If this means, as
the social scientists, the courts, and the Negroes themselves
believe, that this will be the same education my children
have, then I must accept and encourage it.

I must try to see to it that no man be humiliated and
rejected because of his color. If this means that the Negro

eats where I eat, sits next to me in the theatre, or rides next to me in public transportation, then I am obligated to accept it.

I must see to it that every man has an opportunity for a decent home and decent surroundings, and if this means that he will live in my neighborhood or in the house next to mine, then this is the way it must be.

If a Negro wants to worship in my church or join my church, then I am obligated to see to it that he is not only accepted but welcomed into that church, even if it be Trinity Presbyterian Church. I must not be led by false pride to try to judge his motives for coming into that church, and I must welcome any other individual.

I must try to overlook the selfish politicians who use the Negro for their own ends; the Communist agitators who delight in stirring up racial strife; the noisy, aggressive Negro who abuses his privileges and who makes life unpleasant for me; and even the Negroes who exploit their own race. I must ignore such irrelevant matters as which race settled this country, which race pays the most taxes, etc., and remember the basic principles on which I am trying to act and in which I believe.

I must not only accept the efforts of the Negro to achieve his legitimate aspirations, but I must try to help him achieve them, and I believe that the church must do the same if it is a truly Christian church. I must do this, even if it goes against my deepest prejudices and even though it threatens my superior and isolated position in the community and even though it entails the risk of intermarriage.

Basically, the problem is not one of what I like but of what I know to be right. I must not let my wishes determine my attitude toward my associates, my school, my church, or even my own family, but if I am true to the principles which I profess, then I must act according to those principles. THIS I BELIEVE.

Part Three

CLEANSING THAT WHICH IS WITHIN

Ye blind guides, which strain at a gnat, and swallow a camel. Woe unto you, scribes and Pharisees, hypocrites! for ye make clean the outside of the cup and of the platter, but within they are full of extortion and excess.

Thou blind Pharisee, cleanse first that which is within the cup and platter, that the outside of them may be clean also.

—Matthew 23:24–26

Part Three

CHANGING THAT
WHICH IS WITHIN

Chapter 9

BUT WHAT CAN WE DO?

*And let us not be weary in well doing: for in due
season we shall reap, if we faint not.*

—Galatians 6:9

If you have read William Shirer's *Rise and Fall of the Third
Reich*, you will recall mention of German Christians, "from
the old conservative classes," who were revolted by Hitler's
racism and asked Mr. Shirer, "But what can we do?" Mr.
Shirer said that he heard the question frequently, and that it
was not an easy one to answer.

The same question is frequently asked in America. But the
answer is not so difficult to find here, because our government—at least the federal part—does not collaborate with the
racist. And although our government's justice to Negroes has
seemed, at times, to be grinding "exceeding slow," it has at
the same time been grinding exceedingly sure.

What can we do? Well, there is no one easy answer.
Thomas Edison, when asked to describe genius, said it was
98 per cent perspiration and 2 per cent inspiration. This is
about the way it works in human-relations endeavors, too.
You just have to roll up your sleeves and go to work. But
some methods are more effective than others and I give you
an outline of procedures which have been effective for me
and my family.

I don't mean to imply that I have all the answers—far from
it. I just know what has worked for us, and the sharing of
ideas can often be of mutual benefit.

HIRE

One thing you can do, if you are in a position to do it, is to
make a special effort to hire people without regard to their
race or their religion. After hiring them, promote them on
the same basis. If this were done, probably most other race-
related problems would fade away. Money and the good life
it makes possible may not be the most important thing in
the world, but it is up toward the top of the list. How important is it to you? Try to observe the Golden Rule in your
hiring practices as well as in other ways.

VOTE

One of the first things we did after arriving in Little Rock
was to vote and support political action groups. Our first votes
for governor were for Governor Faubus. We certainly did not
enjoy watching the spectacle of three candidates all trying to
outdo the others in their timeworn appeals to prejudice. But
Faubus seemed the most moderate of the three, and so we
voted for him. By 1958 the Governor had become a symbol
of racism and seemed to have changed his position. So we
voted against him. But we really did not have much choice
as the other candidates seemed to concentrate on convincing
voters they could do a better job of preserving segregation
than Faubus. It has been like this in each succeeding election.

I've wondered what might have happened if just one of
Faubus' opponents had said, "Look, folks, racial prejudice is

wrong. Our country is supposed to stand for equal rights and opportunity for all its citizens. No power, domestic or foreign, has yet been able successfully to defy the United States of America, and I doubt if they are about to start now. At least let us hope that they do not. It may take a little time for full compliance with the various court orders, but we will all be better off if we show that we are moving in the direction of compliance. Let us concentrate on good citizenship and Christian ethics in what we proudly call the Bible Belt."

I know that there are still some politicians who would consider such an attitude, and the revelation of it, political suicide. But names such as Clements, Kefauver, Gore, Morton, Sanford, Sanders, and Combs give us hope that the days of the demagogue are numbered.

Although Governor Faubus is still with us, work done by political action groups in Little Rock has made its impact. Moderates have won just about every local election that counted in Little Rock in recent years. Winning these elections was the result of a lot of hard work, doorbell ringing and handshaking by such groups as the S.T.O.P. ("Stop This Outrageous Purge") committee, and the Women's Emergency Committee. All of this work probably even had an effect upon the Governor. During his final television speech of the 1962 campaign he said that he was striving for an Arkansas with equal opportunity for all, regardless of race, creed or color. And later, after the election, he remarked that it was obvious the people did not want a Governor who wandered "in the thickets of extremism."

Participating in political action groups was a new experience for us. We seldom voted in the so-called minor contests such as school-board elections prior to 1955. We have missed none since. We even went from house to house soliciting votes, and helped in telephone work.

Not long ago a former associate, a railroad man from Nebraska, was visiting in Little Rock. I asked him who the governor of Nebraska was. He didn't know! He did say that he thought the fellow was a Democrat! At first I thought he must be kidding, but finally realized he was absolutely sincere. All of this was difficult to believe, until I remembered we might have had the same problem had we just come from Iowa. We have experienced democracy in action, in Little Rock, and have often wished people elsewhere could get as worked up over the "minor" elections as we have.

So there is one thing you can do to fight race prejudice, even in Mississippi (if you are white). Vote!

JOIN AND GIVE

You can join and support organizations dedicated to working for human rights. There are many such groups. The thing to do is align yourself with one or more of them, as your time permits. Join the organizations which seem to concentrate on the particular phase of the human rights struggle most suited to your talent and interests.

The Southern Regional Council is a South-wide organization and the Arkansas branch is known as the Arkansas Council on Human Relations. It is made up largely of business and professional men, educators, and ministers, of both races. They have done what they could to help the community adjust to the various social changes in Arkansas, which were the result of school and other desegregation. One of their most effective programs has been called "Bridges across the Barriers." This started in the fall of 1961 and was done, as they put it, to let the colored children know that not all white people were against them. The Council asked white families to act as advisers, with a white family assigned to each colored family who had a child in an integrated school. We were asked to participate and were glad to help. Knowing people and sharing their problems makes it difficult to "pass by on the other side" when help is needed. I highly recommend personal involvement. If you are not motivated when you start, you will be soon afterwards. The colored girl we were asked to provide guidance for was a senior in Central High in the 1962–63 school year. She is a fine girl, and has adjusted well to situations at Central. Through the help of one of our friends, she got work in the University Hospital in the summer of 1963, and through the help of other friends, she was able to attend college and will eventually become a nurse. It is because of this personal involvement that my wife and I now think of what discrimination does to this particular girl, our friend, rather than just what it does to Negroes in general. In considering how to get her to college, a trip of about three hundred miles, we decided upon an automobile trip to the school. But it suddenly occurred to us that we might not be able to go into a café with her and eat lunch—that she would have to sit outside in the car, while we could walk right in. Thoughts like these give a white person just an inkling, I suppose, of what segregation is like.

LETTERS TO THE EDITOR

I used to think the letters to the editor, published in about half our newspapers, were an effective method of molding public opinion. But after reading these epistles in Little Rock's dailies for the past several years I doubt their value. Most of the letters published in both Little Rock papers have something to do with integration. Those in the *Gazette* have seemed to run about half pro and half con. The *Democrat's* letters ran about 95 per cent for segregation, some being very extreme in their views. This is not surprising as editorials in the *Democrat* sound just about like their letters to the editor, blasting the Kennedys, civil rights, Negro "agitators," etc.

The *Democrat* does not, however, go all the way in follow-

ing the segregationist line. In 1959, when it appeared we
might lose our public schools, the *Democrat* suddenly went
moderate, and advocated law and order, and counseled against
the teacher purge. I heard several staunch segregationists
grumbling about this, and heard remarks such as "I knew we
had lost when the *Democrat* let us down. At least we always
knew where the *Gazette* stood."

What the *Democrat* has done is pretty much what the
Governor has done—told the people exactly what it appeared
the majority wanted to hear. This sells newspapers, but it is
hardly courageous journalism.

I used to believe that letters decrying prejudice might do
more good in the *Democrat* than they would if published in
the *Gazette*. When you want to make converts, you go to the
"mission field." So I sent some letters to the editor of the
Democrat. I soon noticed that each letter published had what
I considered the punch lines deleted. When I complained
about this the editor wrote that it was necessary to limit the
length of letters because of limited space. I felt that this was
reasonable, except that they always managed to cut out what
I felt were my most effective arguments. What was left often
produced exactly the opposite from what I had hoped to get
across. So I gave up on the *Democrat*. I suspect this is what
others who share my beliefs have done.

I have not been a frequent writer of letters to newspapers,
in any event. But I have written several to the *Gazette*. Since
it has become obvious that serious and thoughtful letters do
little good, this leaves about two approaches—satire and humor. My first attempts were satirical. I said that segregation
was all right, but that perhaps we had not gone far enough.
I suggested legislation that would also segregate people according to their incomes and their wealth. I went on to point out
that poor people often live in the worst part of town, are more
likely to steal, become involved in other crimes, have body
odor, and get low grades in school than well-to-do people. I

made it quite clear that this whole setup was contingent upon the dividing line being set up so that I was not grouped with the peons. This letter brought forth a flood of letters denouncing me. So help me, most of those doing the protesting did not get the point! They thought it was a shame that anyone would want to discriminate against a fellow American just because of his financial status. They wondered how I would feel if I were in the segregated group and stated, furthermore, that America was not a place where ideas such as mine would find acceptance. Believe it or not, several of those who wrote in denouncing me were the same people who wrote in before and since defending racial segregation. Finally, one fellow wrote a letter of explanation. He told the Biblical story of King David's indescretion with Bathsheba, and how David had arranged to have Uriah eliminated so David could court the girl with a clear conscience. But the prophet Nathan stood right up to David and told him a story about a rich fellow who had a whole flock of sheep, while a poor, hardworking shepherd had just one little ewe lamb, and ole moneybags took the one little ewe lamb away from the poor hard working shepherd, which left him ewe-less. Nathan asked David what he thought of such a caper, and David said anyone who would pull a stunt like that wasn't fit to eat with the pigs, or something to that effect. Then Nathan stared right at David and said icily, "Thou art the man!" The letter writer said I should have signed my letter Nathan. The letters of protest stopped suddenly.

The humorous letters seem to be most effective. We must keep things light and gay. Negroes can be shot from ambush. Their churches can be burned and bombed. Negroes can be ridiculed and humiliated, but we mustn't get too serious about it.

One of my letters to the editor of the *Gazette*, June 15, 1963, read as follows, under the three-column head, "Warming Up the Old 'Carney' Pitch":

To the Editor of the Gazette:

Those of us who grew up in small towns can easily recall the carnival wrestlers who came to town and stood in front of their tents, beating upon their chests as they challenged all of the "local yokels." We all were aware that the harangues we heard were just so much hot air, and we knew that under their colorful cloaks the shouting gladiators were really old, and paunchy, and probably could not beat their way out of a paper bag. But we suckers always snapped at the bait, paid our quarters, and lined up to get inside the tent and cheer our fair-haired challenger on.

Nowadays we don't have to stand out in the hot sun for all of this. All we need do is pick up a paper and read about our own gladiator as he warms up for his sixth gubernatorial campaign. Like the carnival wrestler, he does little but roar and keep the people stirred up. We know this, and he knows it, but it makes a good show so everyone pretends to be deadly serious. Some of us actually fall for the "come on," even after the fifth time around.

Our hero will start out slowly, by calling the President's speeches ridiculous. Then he will get on the subject of restrooms, as he tells the "Boys' Staters" about girls in Washington having to go to rest rooms in pairs, which brings to mind his accusations in 1957 about soldiers following girls into rest rooms, and we wonder if maybe the fellow has a rest room complex.

By next spring and summer he will pull out all the stops, and be telling us to look into the sweet faces of our innocent grandchildren, and by then we will all be so excited, and mad, at somebody, or something, that we will gladly pay our quarters to get inside the tent, and see the same old sordid show again.

Ralph Creger
Little Rock

I got a lot of favorable comment on this one. As I said, nearly everyone enjoys a good laugh. This is why these letters are the most effective. But there was one fellow who writes to the editors of both Little Rock papers at least three times a week, or so it seems, and he commented in a critical vein about my letter. He said he wanted me to know that Governor Faubus could be elected anytime he decided to run. This, of course, was just the point I was trying to make. So, I repeat, letters to the editor are of doubtful value!

Chapter 10

WHAT CAN WE SAY?

In conservative, evangelical churches the term "personal work" is well known. It refers to those who are zealous enough in their faith to go and talk directly to people about their souls. The theory is advanced that these efforts are much more effective than any number of "dynamic" sermons and more likely to get results than stacks of literature. No doubt this is true. If it is true in the field of evangelism, it can be equally effective for those fighting racial discrimination. Anyone not completely anti-social can become a power to be reckoned with—just by talking!

The experiences of my family in Little Rock the past eight years may or may not be typical for a racial liberal. But they seem to provide some of the answers to the question "But what can we say?"

Our social life is largely church-oriented. Friends we meet socially are usually the same people we see in church, and there are a good many of them. Others in our church tell us they have had the same experience. Even so, we have met many people because of our work in the human relations field, through civic groups, and because of business relationships. So we know a lot of people. We enjoy being with people, enjoy listening, and enjoy talking. Nearly everyone we know understands how we feel about the race issue, and has, with very few exceptions, respected our opinion—even when he did not agree. We had expected some antagonism because of our so-called Yankee origin. (We did not know we were Yankees until our arrival in Arkansas—we thought Yankees came from New England.) Oddly enough, there has been little reference made to our background, even by some of our friends who are pretty strong segregationists. I think this is because they know we are sincere about our convictions. It isn't too difficult to spot the phony. We like Arkansas, it is our home, and I think this is obvious to our friends.

When talking to people about racial matters we readily admit that people in the North are just as susceptible to racial prejudice (but no more so) as southerners. We usually can agree that when there is so much that needs to be done *everywhere* in the field of human relations, it's pretty silly to bicker over which region does the best job of combating prejudice. And we have heard the idea suggested, more than once, that the theory that one must display prejudice as evidence of regional loyalty is an insult to the many fine southerners who have taken the lead in combating racial discrimination. Trying automatically to associate prejudice with the South is a defense mechanism of some of the people in the North who may have a little bit of a guilt complex, and it is also the last weapon of frustrated racists in the South, who think they can enlist support by continually replaying that broken record, "Why Is Everybody Always Pickin' on Me?"

We certainly do not confine our conversation to racial matters when we are with friends. As a matter of fact, we talk mostly about water skiing, current events of national interest, our children, and our church. But just about anyone can get the opportunity, sooner or later, to say what he thinks about prejudice, intolerance, and demagogic politicians.

DISAGREE WITHOUT BEING DISAGREEABLE

To be effective, you must be able to disagree without being disagreeable. Remember that you can no more win an argument about segregation than you can win one on religion. One of the phrases which rolls automatically off the tongues of segregationists is "Trying to shove this down our throats." So bear this in mind when in a group where segregationists are present and avoid broaching the subject of race. Rest assured that sooner or later the segregationist will try to shove his ideas *down your throat*. Then you will be in a position for an effective rebuttal because you didn't start it.

Even then, it is very important that you never let the discussion degenerate into a shouting match. Never forget that as one dedicated to tolerance, you must be tolerant of others —including segregationists. Some will not extend the same courtesy to you, but others will. We have friends who feel nearly as strongly in favor of segregation as we feel against it. We have solved the problem by saying in effect, "There are about ninety-nine things we agree on to the one we do not, so why fall out over that one?"

You might win a friend to your point of view but you will never win an enemy. And if a man elects not to accept my point of view, I still want to be his friend if he will let me.

RETAIN YOUR SENSE OF HUMOR

In your talks with people about prejudice it is important that you retain your sense of humor. If you don't have one to start with it might be best to forget the whole business of trying to win moderates and influence segregationists. The segregationists are usually well fortified with jokes about Negroes.

Sometimes I have wondered if they didn't feel that maybe, if they laughed hard enough at and about Negroes, integration would go away. So it is well to be prepared to take a lot of ribbing after you have made your position clear. The important thing is to relax and have a good time; to be able to dish it out as well as take it in the humor department. This should not be too difficult as the things racists do and say are often far more ridiculous than the grammatical errors and other mistakes some Negroes make.

So try to get in a few jokes about racists when you are at a party and someone asks, "Did you hear the one about the ole nigger preacher?" or, "Did you hear the one about the colored gal who . . . ?" It seems that stories which ridicule Negroes can be decidedly risqué and still be quite acceptable in what passes for polite society. An equal degree of indecency in stories about the white folks would likely be frowned upon by the gnat-strainers. But these are not happy people anyway, so don't worry about them. You want your parties to have balance. Anyway, most people are not going to give you much trouble when they are laughing with you, or at you.

So the next time you are with the gang, ask them if they have heard the story about the Negro organization which had managed to persuade a bus company in Alabama to hire a few Negro bus drivers. The local White Citizens Council blocked this move, though, until they had received assurance that all of the steering wheels would be at least twenty-five feet long!

And of course, James Meredith can get into the act. It seems some of the Ole Miss students conceived the idea of letting him go out for football practice, figuring that the linemen would take good care of James. Mr. Meredith was given the ball, but instead of meeting an untimely death, he squirmed, stiff-armed, twisted and dodged, got into the open, and outran everyone for eighty yards to the goal line. "Wow," screamed the coach to an aide. "Look at that Indian run!"

If you really want to jolt someone, tell him about the

strongly segregationist senator who discovered that an aide
from the home state was going about with a comely colored
girl who worked in the Pentagon. The senator started to give
the young fellow quite a tongue-lashing, but the young man
countered, "Just a cotton-pickin' minute, Senator, I don't
want to go to school with the girl, I just want to marry her!"

There are many of these tales which may, or may not be
true. That is not important. The important thing is to
see that you do not let the segregationists have a monopoly
on the belly laugh. And in recent years I have noticed that
Citizens Council leaders have been butts of jokes about as
often as "old nigger preachers." It should not be too difficult
to steer the humor in the right direction.

A TIME TO SPEAK, AND A TIME TO REMAIN SILENT

There are times to speak and times to remain silent. One
night as we were in a social gathering and one of the men
started to tell a standard Negro joke, another member of the
party reminded him that we might not be as appreciative as
expected. But the humorist continued, after explaining that
some of his best friends were Negroes. He said it is a known
fact that all Negroes have a weakness for trying to use big
words, the meaning of which is far beyond their comprehen-
sion. (The previous night we had been at a meeting sponsored by the Arkansas Council on Human Relations and had
heard several colored high school students speak with great
poise and ability, using words I am sure they understood, but
which our storyteller might not have. These same students
later won national recognition for their academic achievements.) The storyteller continued, with a lengthy disserta-
tion about an old "Nigra" (Nigra for my benefit) preacher
who did not want his church to spend money for a new

chandelier "because they needed a light fixture worse," and besides, "no one would know how to play it."

I looked at Barbara and I knew she was thinking about the kids speaking the previous night, and we smiled, and everyone thought we were sharing their joke. And so everyone was happy. The point is that some people are willing, even anxious, to hear about the various aspects of the Negro's rapid gains in the field of education, but others don't want to discuss it. You have to know the difference in the people, because it's a waste of time trying to get into the matter with folks whose minds are closed. You do nothing but antagonize them.

There are many things you can discuss when talking to people, and get in a plug for justice. A lot of current movies, books, and television shows have a human-rights theme, and it is easy to mention these commonly discussed subjects; the other fellow will often mention them first. National television features many sports programs in which it is obvious that the Negro is doing a pretty fair job in a situation where he competes because of merit. The movie *To Kill a Mockingbird* is an outstanding picture. The main theme is not race, but sometimes the point is made better when it is not advertised. I could not help but think about the mob that Atticus faced, and how it was about certain that the men in the mob would all have voted for George Wallace, while Atticus would have been pretty likely to vote against him. But the Atticuses have been outnumbered in the past. In discussing this movie with friends, we found everyone agreed that he would rather be an Atticus.

Judgment at Nuremburg made considerable impact, too. Many people were quite aware of an obvious analogy. For those who were not, we filled in the details. In the movie, the American judge, played by Spencer Tracy, was discussing Nazi racism with a kindly German friend. The German, as many others had done before him, discounted any knowledge of persecution against Jews. He said he certainly had participated in none of the alleged atrocities and that he thought a lot of it was "imagined," a result of distortions by the press. He said the Americans would be better advised to check up a little more closely on the communists, as the Germans had done so effectively. There might have been a few hoodlums who participated in some harmless pranks, he agreed, but the good people of Germany did not condone such acts, and did not participate.

THREE THINGS TO EMPHASIZE WITH SEGREGATIONISTS

At least half of our conversations about desegregation have been with people who held moderate views. But we have not neglected our segregationist friends. The approach with these people is necessarily different. When talking to segregationists our efforts at persuasion have been concentrated in three general areas:

1. THE CHRISTIAN APPROACH: It does no good to try and discount the arguments of the strong segregationists since the various deficiencies they believe inherent in Negroes are, to them, not open to question. The racist's mind is closed on this subject. But you can tell these people that even if they are right about the inferiority of Negroes, this still does not alter Christ's teachings about how to treat our fellow men. Christ's "Do ye therefore unto others . . ." was not based on the IQ, body odor, per capita income, or personal appearance of the "others." Christ simply said, "Therefore, all things whatsoever ye would that men should do unto you, do ye even so to them." Emphasize this when talking to segregationists.

2. INEVITABILITY: Even the most ardent segregationist will tell you dourly, "It's coming." Well, then, we say, if it's com-

ing, or if it is already here, how are we to behave? Should we behave as good citizens are supposed to behave toward other citizens, and behave as Christians; or should we act like barbarians?

3. SEGREGATION BREEDS PROTEST: Because of my writing I have visited some of Little Rock's all-Negro schools and some of the Negro churches. I noticed that the schoolteachers and the preachers were the same people I had seen in other meetings, urging civil rights. There have been many newspaper accounts of Negro youngsters "spilling out" of Negro schools to join in the various protest marches and demonstrations. They do not "spill out" of integrated schools for this purpose. For the most part it has been students from Negro colleges who have staged the sit-ins, the kneel-ins and the protest marches. Right or wrong it seems that the colored young people get a lot more encouragement to demand their citizenship rights when in Negro schools, and with Negro teachers, than they do in integrated schools. This is something for the segregationist to think about. We have seen that he does.

DEALING WITH THE CLICHÉ-MAKERS

Everyone who has incurred the wrath of racists knows that there are many cliché-makers among them. You don't have to read many letters to the editor in papers catering to racists to pick out these hackneyed phrases without which the letters would be dull indeed. Let us examine three of the most commonly used labels:

1. "NIGGER LOVER." If this is the kind of love the Bible talks about—compassion, and respect for your fellow man— tell your accusers you plead guilty.

2. "DO-GOODER." This is another nebulous term. Surely, it is better to do good than to do evil. When they start calling racists "do-gooders," or accuse them of doing good, then we'd

better begin to worry. So if they call you a "do-gooder," just say, "Listen, bub, flattery will get you nowhere!"

3. "FUZZY-MINDED INDIVIDUAL." This one is really "way out." I think it means that the accused doesn't know his own mind. If this is correct, then I deny categorically that I am the least bit "fuzzy." Like Fuzzy Wuzzy, the bear, who wasn't fuzzy, wuzzy? By golly, I wasn't fuzzy either! In fact, I am convinced that my mind is much clearer on the subject of prejudice than the fellow who starts his letter to the editor thusly, "Now I don't try to force my way into a country club, why do n—?"

The thing you must remember is that most of the cliché-makers are not going to change their thinking, and wouldn't, even if God took them up on a mountain and wrote the rules on a piece of rock. So don't worry about the name-callers. If you cannot resist using labels too, try the term "camel-swallower," ["They stood there, wearing their little beanies, with their girl friends by their sides, and called us every filthy name in the book"[1]] or "gnat-strainer." ["These are a deeply religious people, they would never tolerate or forgive the registering of James Meredith on a Sunday."[1]]

WHO ARE THE PREJUDICED?

A seemingly successful approach when talking to moderates is one I have frequently used in church and other discussion groups. In these conversations the pros and cons of segregation versus integration were avoided. Rather, we asked ourselves, "Who are the people likely to be prejudiced?" Well, even in groups where there were people inclined toward segregation, there was general agreement with the following axiomatic statements:

[1] From press reports about the happenings at the University of Mississippi when a lone Negro Mississippian enrolled.

1. Educated people are less prone to race prejudice than the uneducated. (Nearly all of the people I have met in the various human rights groups in Little Rock have been college graduates. On the other hand, the people I know who have less than a high school education are nearly all strong segregationists.)

2. Religious people are less inclined toward race prejudice than the irreligious. (This is in spite of all I have been saying about the timidity of preachers and church leaders. Most of these people know "in their hearts" segregation is wrong. Many of the leaders in the human rights groups are preachers.)

3. Successful people are less inclined toward prejudice than the unsuccessful. (There are exceptions to this, of course, but, basically, successful people do not have the problem of trying to find someone inferior to them.)

4. Old people are more likely to be prejudiced than the young. (Youth can be cruel at times—but they also are willing to accept change. They can surprise you with their sense of justice and desire for fair play. Young people of both races have assumed the leadership in efforts to erase racial barriers.)

There are exceptions to all of these rules, but the people in our discussion groups have agreed that these conclusions are fundamentally correct. After they reached the conclusions, all there was left for them to do was to classify themselves. For some reason they invariably turned out to be quite liberal about the matter of racial prejudice and segregation.

In discussions with people who seem to be honestly concerned about matters pertaining to prejudice and its ramifications a thorough study of commonly used (and misused) words can be very helpful.

There are a lot of words being bandied about because of racial tension. The meaning of these words seems obscure to many people. In some parts of America politicians have succeeded in making "integration" a dirty word. In other parts of our land the same can be said for the word "segregation." Governor Faubus, who has never yet made public his secret as to whether he is a segregationist or an integrationist, has been quite successful in frightening people by calling them integrationists. When things have gotten particularly difficult for the Governor, he has pulled out all the stops and called his opponents hard-core integrationists. I think we liberals have made a mistake in getting upset over such accusations. The thing to do, it seems to me, is to surprise him and reply, "OK. So I'm a hard-core integrationist. You are a demagogue. What about it?"

CHECK YOUR DICTIONARY

The real issue is not confined to words, but to ideas. And the big question is, should we deny Negroes their basic human rights, or should we not? Try to confine your discussions to this issue. Don't let the racists cloud the issue with a lot of undefined labels if you can help it. But regardless of your efforts the words may continue to pop up. So it would be well to make a thorough study of the most frequently used word in the segregation controversy. Check your dictionary. Here are some of the most commonly used terms:

Hard-core Integrationist.
Definition, word by word:
Hard: Not easily penetrated, firm, solid, earnest, persevering.
Core: The central part.
Integrate: To become united so as to form a complete or perfect whole. Judging from these definitions, the hard-core integrationist is not the ogre pictured by the demagogic politician.
Segregate: To separate or to cut off from others. To isolate.

To seclude. (I wouldn't want these things done to me. I don't want to do them to others.)

Bigot: One obstinately attached to some creed, opinion, or practice so as to be illiberal or intolerant.

Demagogue: A leader who seeks to make capital of social discontent and gain political influence.

Prejudice: Preconceived judgment or opinion. Unreasonable predilection or objection. An opinion or leaning adverse to anything without just grounds or before sufficient knowledge.

Conservative: Disposed to maintain existing institutions or views. Opposed to change. (This could be good or bad depending upon the institution or view you are talking about.)

Liberal: Not narrow or contracted in mind. Independent in opinion. Having a tendency toward democratic or republican as distinguished from aristocratic or monarchical forms of government.

Explaining the meaning of these frequently misused words can do much to clear the air and eliminate misunderstandings.

Chapter 11

WHAT CAN WE WRITE?

I am sure the average person would think it unlikely that he could write something and then get it published. But let me tell you of some of my experiences. Because of them, I am now convinced that just about anyone who has a reasonable amount of ability can (and will), if he wants, achieve something worthwhile in the field of literature *providing* he feels strongly enough about his subject matter. If he is concerned enough, he will manage to find the words.

Opportunities for writing sometimes present themselves in strange ways.

For example, in 1959, my son Carl, along with other Central High American History students, was required to write a term paper on any subject of his choosing pertaining to history. Carl asked me for advice, and I suggested he write on the history of the Negro in America. We checked with the history instructor to ask if it would be permissible to collaborate and were given permission. The teacher told me he wished more parents took a similar attitude, and that he was sure he would be "on the list" if the Governor ever undertook another "teacher purge." When we completed the composition we showed it to friends, who turned out to be most enthusiastic and insisted the story should be published as a small book. Through the help of these friends and by contacting several nationally known people I felt would be sympathetic to my position, the essay we had prepared as "An American Success Story" was accepted for publication by a New York publisher, and the title was changed to *This Is What We Found.*

In the book we tried to employ a new approach to the race problem, as we felt it pointless to bring out all the old and hackneyed arguments most of us have heard so many times on both sides of the issue. It seemed to us that one of the most important aspects in the Negro's battle for full citizenship, one that has not been fully exploited, has been the admiration that just about anyone, if he is human at all, has for others able to achieve success despite handicaps. And even the most bigoted segregationist must admit, if he is honest, that Negroes have been handicapped.

Although we were as active as we knew how to be the first few years we lived in Little Rock, working for equal rights, there is no doubt that the chance classroom assignment for Carl, and the subsequent publication of our book, increased our zeal. It was nice to get the recognition that we got, and we were particularly pleased with the number of calls and letters we got which commended us for our stand. If nothing else, our book's acceptance showed people who wanted to be shown that they no longer had to be afraid. We did get two crank telephone calls and some anonymous letters. One of them contained a card bearing these printed words: "For your part in helping to integrate the Little Rock schools I hereby make you an honorary 'nigger.'" I think that this was a card, fictitiously signed T. Marshall, left over from the many sent out to Little Rock people who had been working to reopen the schools in 1959, and I am sure such cards are expected to strike terror into the heart of the recipient. If the sender had seen the laughs it evoked at various social gatherings he'd no doubt have put in an immediate call to the KKK Klavern for further instructions. The tragic part of what happened in

Little Rock, though, was that for a short time the senders of such cards were calling the shots.

This sort of climate is certainly not what most people would want for their community, and it seemed to me that its existence was partly the fault of the church's silence. It seemed the church had been weighed in the balance and found wanting. I did more writing on the subject of race prejudice and what follows is typical. A lot of people who want to combat racism do not have the time or inclination to write, but the same pleas I used can be used in daily conversations, at work, at parties, in schools, and above all in the churches. A church friend who read my article came to me to talk about it. He told me that he knew he was prejudiced, that he always had been, and was trying his best to get rid of his prejudice. But, he admitted, it was not easy for him. I felt very humble about all this, since I had my own prejudice, and I knew that there were times I was quite "intolerant." Since I could do no more than my friend, and do what I could to shed my prejudices, the only reply I could think of was, "Welcome to the club!"

The article that my church friend commented on was published in the *Arkansas Baptist Newsmagazine* and was reprinted in the *Arkansas Gazette* and in other newspapers and magazines. It read as follows:

> *BLAND LEADING THE BLAND?*
> *. . . "TO ONE OF THE LEAST OF THESE . . ."*
> By Ralph Creger
> Deacon in Calvary [Baptist] Church, Little Rock
> Then one of them, which was a lawyer, asked him a question, tempting him, and saying,
> Master, which is the great commandment in the law?
> Jesus said unto him, Thou shalt love the Lord thy God with all thy heart, and with all thy soul, and with all thy mind.
> This is the first and great commandment.

And the second is like unto it, Thou shalt love thy neighbor as thyself.

On these two commandments hang all the law and the prophets.

(Matthew 22:35–40)

Those of us who admit the presence of a problem, and are concerned about it, know that when church leaders are urged to speak out against racial prejudice the most frequent excuse given for silence is that we should concentrate on "preaching the gospel."

Certainly we should never forget that the purpose of the church is to evangelize the world, but we must realize that we can work ever so diligently at saving souls and fail miserably because those we seek to reach will consider us hypocrites if they can see that we obey Christ's "Second Great Commandment" only when it is convenient or expedient to obey.

We read in I John 2:4: "He that sayeth, I know him, and keepeth not his commandments, is a liar, and the truth is not in him." Those outside the church may not be familiar with this particular verse of scripture, but they certainly understand the principle involved.

Frankly, I have reasons other than religious for opposing racial discrimination. I guess the primary reason has to do with pride. This may come as a shock to the racist, who talks a great deal about pride but is really talking about vanity. Anyone with real pride and confidence in himself would not want to force those with whom he competes for grades, jobs, or status to operate under a handicap. They would never want this unless, that is, they have serious doubts about their ability to meet the competition of all other Americans.

WHAT WOULD JESUS DO?

But all of this should be of secondary consideration to the Christian. The problems arising from social changes already here demand attention. The first question we, as Christians, should ask ourselves is, "What would Jesus do?"

As far as Christian behavior is concerned, Christ made it abundantly clear where he placed the emphasis (Matthew 22: 37–39). So it is increasingly hard to understand why so many who call themselves Christians ignore "the weightier matters of the law" (Matthew 23:23), straining at doctrinal gnats while eagerly swallowing the very large camel of racial prejudice.

Silence on race issues, by church people, grows more and more difficult to explain as we search the scriptures. For acts of prejudice and unequal treatment to people because of their race is in conflict with just about everything Christ taught about human relations. They certainly are in conflict with his second great commandment and his Golden Rule. And they are in conflict with the royal law (James 2:2–10) which warns against having "respect to persons," and instructing people, according to status: "Sit here in a good place," "Stand thou there," or "Sit here, under my footstool."

I think anyone really honest about the matter would admit that the last thing he would want would be to be treated as Negroes have been treated in America for so many years.

Here, in this Christian nation, we see Negroes jailed, spat at, cursed, legislated against, ridiculed and threatened with loss of jobs for simply making it clear they want to share equally in their country's citizenship rights and for demonstrating that they would like to share equally in the blessings of Christ's commandments. That these things have happened is the shame of the Bible Belt.

Ross Coggins, of the Christian Life Commission of the Southern Baptist Convention, says in his booklet, "Missions and Race": "Missionaries believe they have a right to expect this note (against racial discrimination) to be sounded with courage from pulpits here in America. Needless to say, they are often bitterly disappointed. Their courage in going to the ends of the earth is often unmatched by Christian leaders at home who blandly ignore the existence of a problem. In the chaotic world of today, can the bland lead the bland?"

Billy Graham counsels frequently against the "sin of racial prejudice." He states simply, "Jim Crow must go." But the vast majority of church leaders seem willing to gloss over the hypocritical perversion of an integral part of the gospel we have been told to proclaim.

I have talked to several ministers about how racial prejudice is in conflict with Christ's teachings. Nearly all of them, after seeing that they could not evade the issue, admitted that prejudice is wrong but tried to justify silence by pointing out that straight talk might offend some of their congregation. They mention dismissal of ministers who have refused to be silenced.

But what sort of Christianity is this? Would to God we had more "servants of Christ" who had the courage to say, as Paul said, "As we said before, so say I now again, If any man preach any other gospel unto you than that ye have received, let him be accursed. For do I now persuade men, or God? or do I seek to please men? for if I yet pleased men, I should not be the servant of Christ" (Gal. 1:9–10).

CRUEL HYPOCRISY

I suppose the cruel hypocrisy of all these things looms larger to one personally acquainted with many of the colored young people who have been in the front lines of the Negro's struggle for entry into the main stream of American life. Because of a book on race written by my son and me, my family was asked by the Arkansas Council on Human Relations to help some of the youngsters entering predominantly white schools. I feel that we have grown spiritually and in understanding because of our experiences.

We were told that most of the Negro students were Christian and active in their churches, and that many of them were deeply hurt because of the actions of so many white people they had assumed to be Christian. We, as well as many other white families, resolved to do what we could to let these young people know that God is "still in his heaven," even though things are obviously not "right with the world."

We have considered it a great privilege to know such young people as Jacquelyne Evans, Hall High "A-plus" honor student; Frank Henderson, a minister's son whose friendly personality did much to ease tensions in Central High in 1959; Sybil Jordan, Central High graduate who received a large scholarship grant because of her academic achievements; Myrna Davis, East Side Junior High student, who has a real talent for writing; and Gloria Nelson, Central High senior, who aspires to a career in nursing.

We have been pleasantly surprised at the number of people ready to help us in our efforts to help Gloria get some kind of a college scholarship so that she can realize her ambition to become a nurse. We have been amazed at the dedication, the quiet determination and lack of bitterness of these and many other colored young people in Little Rock. They will do well. It could happen, as Harry Golden would say, "only in America."

While there have been many aspects of Little Rock's reaction to the appeals of demagogues in 1957 and since that make one wonder about the effectiveness of the church, we take pride in the young people of Calvary Baptist Church, Little Rock. In 1957 there was a young man in our church who was a student in Central High. He planned to, and has since, entered the ministry. He said that he did not order "de-segregation" but felt that as a Christian he could do no less than practice Christ's Golden Rule in his relationship to the frightened Negro newcomers.

For offering a friendly greeting and for sitting down to eat with the shunned Negroes, this young man was beaten, later, by four hoodlums. He and his family were awakened at night, many times, by threatening, abusive, and obscene telephone calls. But there was no word of encouragement for this boy, or for others like him, from the leadership of most of Little Rock's churches.

CHRISTIANITY AND PREJUDICE

In 1959, after the schools reopened, tensions eased considerably. One day a young man in my Sunday school department came to me and wanted to talk. He said that he could no longer reconcile Christianity which he studied on Sunday with the racial prejudice he saw every other day of the week. As the months passed, other young people voiced similar conclusions.

In 1961 one of our most dedicated young ladies graduated from high school and went on to Ouachita College, in Arkadelphia, to prepare for work as a missionary. At college she joined with other students to help a colored church with their youth program.

This past year the young people of our church presented a play about missions. As there was no advance warning, members of the congregation may have done a "double take" on seeing a colored boy in the cast. Our young people had decided that the obvious choice for a person to portray a colored man was a colored man. The kids got along fine, both on stage and downstairs for refreshments after the play. As to the oldsters, about the only comment of note was heard in the foyer afterwards, "Well, I notice the roof didn't fall in."

LITTLE ROCK PROGRESS

We still hear occasional outbursts of racism, but I think we can be proud of the progress being made in Little Rock. During the awards presentations to the "Ten Outstanding Young Men of 1962," the human rights theme was strongly emphasized by the honorees. A minister, in making his acceptance speech, closed by saying, "You and I will not be free until James Meredith is free!" The huge throng rose in a standing ovation. One of those joining in the demonstration was Arkansas' Governor Faubus.

So, with the young people leading the way, we may be much nearer to the American ideal of justice and the Christian ideal of love than most of us dared to hope, even a few short years ago. I only wish more of my own generation, in the church, had led, rather than followed, in the all-important area of human rights.

In working with young people in the church and in directing "assembly programs," I have tried to avoid placing too much emphasis on race. But I have tried to face the issue when I felt it needed to be discussed. My usual approach is to ask the young people to try to imagine how they would feel to be on the receiving end of what the Negro gets as a steady diet. I have used a plan of stressing six points.

POINT 1. If colored, they could be downtown shopping, become hungry, go to a lunch counter to eat, but be denied service because of race.

POINT 2. They could be doing manual labor, in the suburban area, be thirsty, go to a restaurant for a cold drink and be turned away.

POINT 3. They might be traveling across America, stop at a hotel or a motel and be turned away.

POINT 4. They might be out of work, unable to get a decent job because of a systematic and effective "job ceiling" used against Negroes, and, due to lack of funds, be unable to provide proper clothing for self and family.

POINT 5. In certain states, they might be in an accident, be refused admission at a nearby hospital, taken miles further to a "Negro" hospital, and die because of the unnecessary time consumed.

POINT 6. They might be demonstrating for the simple right to vote, in some states, be thrown in prison, beaten, and attacked by police dogs.

I tell the young people that these things happen because Christians either do nothing or support a system where these things are encouraged, when they vote for "race-baiting" politicians. I emphasize the fact that sins of omission can be as deadly as sins of commission. Then I read from the book of Matthew, Chapter 25, verses 40 through 46:

> And the King shall answer and say unto them, Verily I say unto you, Inasmuch as ye have done it unto one of the least of these my brethren, ye have done it unto me. Then shall he say unto them on the left hand, Depart from me, ye cursed, into everlasting fire, prepared for the devil and his angels: For [1.] I was ahungered, and ye gave me no meat: [2.] I was thirsty, and ye gave me no drink: [3.] I was a stranger, and ye took me not in: [4.] naked, and ye clothed me not: [5.] Sick, [6.] and in prison, and ye visited me not.
>
> Then shall they also answer him, saying, Lord, when saw we thee ahungered, or athirst, or a stranger, or naked, or sick, or in prison, and did not minister unto thee?
>
> Then shall he answer them, saying, Verily I say unto you, Inasmuch as ye did it not to one of the least of these, ye did it not to me.

I have found, after reading these verses aloud, that further comment has been superfluous.

This was the magazine article that seemed to disturb Governor Faubus.

Chapter 12

WHAT CAN WE ANSWER?

In your efforts to persuade, the things that you do, the things that you say, and the things that you write can all be effective, if you are sincere about the things that you do and say and write. Of the three, the things that you say may accomplish the most.

The talking you do can take the form of public speaking, if you have the opportunity and the ability. It may necessarily be confined to group discussions. But wherever and whenever you talk, prepare yourself to answer logically the questions that will be thrown at you by people about racial prejudice and related matters. You can get many of the answers from books obtainable in public libraries. In the Little Rock library I found ninety-eight books on prejudice and social problems. But you will find that your most effective answers do not come from books, but are the result of your personal involvement with the problem.

What follows is a list of questions familiar to all who are used to hearing racists expound their views. In case you should want to refresh your memory, buy a few back copies of any newspaper with a segregationist editorial policy and read their letters to the editor.

These ideas are apt to be presented to you as a statement of fact, rather than as questions. But if a person is actually starting to think seriously and wonder about a lot of previously unquestioned ideas, they may very well be questions. At any rate, I am using a series of questions and answers to explain the arguments I have found to be most successful. Although they do not always break down prejudice, they nearly always break down hostility.

Some of the answers I give are obviously facetious. As to the others, I couldn't be more serious. Some of them are suitable for use at your church brotherhood or missionary circle meeting, while others should be used on the men at the foundry. Some Dr. McDonald wouldn't let me use at all!

But try to select the arguments that fit the occasion. If you aren't enough of a diplomat to do that, just give—don't talk.

Question: Negroes have thick lips and wide noses. Doesn't this prove they descended from apes?

Answer: Since I am a fundamentalist at heart, I don't think that any of us sprang from apes. But what worries me about all this "monkey business" is the realization that if either of us have ape ancestors, it is very likely we white folks. Apes do not have thick lips. They have very thin lips. It is true that they have wide nostrils, but, on the other hand they have hairy chests, arms, and legs. So this makes the score two to one in favor of the Globetrotters.

Bananas, anyone?

Question: The people of Africa have not contributed their proportionate share to the culture and scientific advancement of the world. Isn't this proof of the Negro's inferiority?

Answer: Well, there might be some question about the "advancement." We remember the song, "Bongo, Bongo, Bongo, I don't want to leave the Congo—they have things like the atom bomb, I think I'll stay where I A'hm." So when the button is pressed, I don't know who might seem to be the smart ones.

Seriously, none of the peoples who inhabit the torrid zone around the earth have been able to do a great deal, as long as they remained in this environment, except to stay alive and reproduce. People just don't work much quantitative analysis operating in a sort of steam bath. White people living very long in the torrid zone soon seem to get that tired, run-down feeling, too. And colored peoples coming into more temperate zones seem to be able to acquire their Ph.D.s from major universities rather frequently. But all of this is not relevant to whether we should, or should not, withhold basic citizenship rights from people because of the color of their skin, and because of their race or national origin. We don't restrict Americans of Portuguese descent and give Americans of German descent all the breaks possible just because Germany appears to be the more progressive nation. Of course, if the German happens to have the savvy, and winds up a big success while the Portuguese is running a fruit stand, nobody is going to worry about it, because they both took pot luck, and neither one had the cards stacked against him from the very day of his birth because of something over which he had no control. When people become Americans we judge them on their merit—or at least that's the way it's supposed to be.

Question: Negroes are better off in America and have a higher standard of living than Negroes do in any other country in the world. What are they complaining about?

Answer: Americans of Irish descent have it better than the people of Ireland, Americans of German descent have it better than they do in Germany, Americans of Russian descent have it better than they do in Russia, Americans of English descent have it better than they do in England. Americans of whatever national origin have it better than they would have in the country of their ancestors. So why make such a big thing of it because this also applies to Negroes? This argument would get you nowhere if you were trying to segregate the Irish. And it isn't doing much toward thwarting the Negro's efforts, either.

Question: The people here just won't stand for integration. Don't you agree?

Answer: This is what was told me in Little Rock eight years ago. But the people have done an amazingly good job of standing for it. It is true that when Governor Faubus warned repeatedly that there would be trouble, a few of the faithful obliged him and provided the trouble. But the plaudits and the cheers given Negro honor students in some of Little Rock's integrated schools in recent years indicate that most of the kids really want to be fair, if given the chance. Aside from school desegregation, just about every other public facility in Little Rock has been desegregated. People who vowed they would never sit down at the same lunch counter with Negroes now walk right into the coffee shop in the railroad station where I work and place their orders, although frequently there are colored patrons being served. The old colored waiting room has been abandoned and forgotten and has been converted into an office. Negroes are much in evidence at the public library. When driving to work I have stopped doing double-takes upon seeing Negro golfers tee off at the municipal golf course. Two forlorn-looking white pickets, protesting the desegregating of Little Rock's downtown lunch counters hardly rated a second glance by those passing by. At baseball games, integration created scarcely a ripple, except occasionally when the visiting team's "niggers" gave "our colored boys" a bad time.

It is surprising how little difference desegregation really makes in a way of life. And you can assure those who really value their prejudices that they will not have to give them up. Take the anti-Semites, for example. Jews have always been able to get justice in the courts in America. They have not been segregated in public places. Consequently, they have been able to do pretty well for themselves. But the Jew haters have been able to maintain their old hatreds and prejudices almost intact. The same thing will happen when we stop segregating Negroes. But the Negroes won't really care if a few racists still cling fanatically to their bias. On the other hand, some of them may "cry all the way to the bank."

Question: Don't you think the Negroes are trying to take over the country?

Answer: If a group of people constituting only 10 per cent of our population, who have been exploited for years, who have been poorly educated, poorly trained, and discriminated against at every turn can manage to take over, we'd better let them. Think what they could do to our foreign adversaries. None of the Negroes I know want to take over anything except the same right to "life, liberty and the pursuit of happiness" that I take for granted.

Question: I am proud that I am Scotch-Irish. Why don't the "niggers" have pride in their race?

Answer: If the people in Scotland and Ireland knew how their names were bandied about by racists here in America they might not be very happy about it. But to answer the question: It would seem much more important to have pride in what you have accomplished as an individual than to have pride in something you had nothing to do with. However, any race or group that can produce people like Gloria Richardson, who was unafraid of a whole city; Medgar Evers, who could not be cowed, only killed by the racists in Mississippi; and six- and seven-year-old children willing to brave high-pressure hoses, police dogs, and billy clubs, can be proud—if pride is so all-important.

Segregationists do a lot of talking about standing firm. Three governors did a lot of talking about going to jail for their cause. I have seen none behind bars yet. Where is their pride?

Question: Don't you think Negroes are actually superior in sports?

Answer: Watch out for this one. This is the sort of question now put to you by the fellow who, twenty years ago, said Negroes could never make it in professional sports. The point he wants to make is that there is a big difference—just any kind of difference. Then, if you agree with him, you'll have a difficult time defending the idea that Negroes are not inherently inferior morally, intellectually, or spiritually.

It is true that there are statistics which would tend to prove the Negro superior in athletics. Fifteen years after the barrier was broken, 18 per cent of the players in professional baseball were colored. A check of charts showing batting averages, runs batted in, and home runs hit provides an even stronger jolt. Willie Mays is the highest paid player in baseball. Wilt (the Stilt) Chamberlain is the highest salaried basketball player in America, and Jimmy Brown rates the biggest wage in football. Negroes have had a monopoly on boxing championships for the past generation. As soon as they let her in the club-houses, Althea Gibson proceeded to win all the women's tennis championships in the world. And so it goes. But in spite of all this superficial evidence, I still do not feel that Negroes have an inherent athletic superiority. I believe a colored athlete at the Rome Olympics hit the nail right on the head. When asked by a reporter why there were so many Negroes on America's team, the young man said simply, "We're hungrier."

Question: How much longer do you think we will be having serious racial trouble in America?

Answer: Not much longer, I hope. My reasoning is that most Americans are realists. More than this, our people have reached the point where they do not need to grasp at the psychological crutch of race-caste in order to fortify their egos.

Question: My Negro maid tells me she doesn't want any part of this integration business, and that she doesn't want her kids in the white schools. What do you think about that?

Answer: Well, I think you'd better check up on your maid. She probably has her kids lined up for next week's sit-in. If she is, in fact, content to be segregated, that's fine. She and her family will probably have no trouble at all in keeping themselves isolated, if they really want to. But what about the other fellow's maid, or the colored schoolteacher, or preacher, or lawyer, who wants the best schooling possible for his kids, at the best possible public school? What if they have children above average in talent or intelligence who want an even break on job opportunities? What if these other Negroes don't like to be segregated in public places? What about them? Should we restrict their progress and their right to life, liberty, and the pursuit of happiness just because of their color?

Question: The Negroes used to be carefree and happy before these agitators got them all stirred up. Why couldn't people let well enough alone?

Answer: It wasn't well enough. You can usually tell how people feel by the songs they sing. For decades, when they were not able to express themselves more forcefully, Negroes sang: "Lonesome Road," "Let My People Go," "Swing Low, Sweet Chariot," and "Nobody Knows the Trouble I've Seen."

Question: Why are people in the South friendlier than people in the North?

Answer: They aren't. They may have a slightly different way of expressing their friendship, but I have adopted a policy of stressing how very similar all Americans really are. I can recall countless instances in Iowa when a farmer became ill and could not harvest his crops and was treated to the heartwarming experience of seeing his neighbors come from miles around to do his work. And this is exactly what the farmers in Arkansas would do under similar circumstances. I have a feeling it would happen in New Hampshire, too. No one region of the country has a monopoly on friendship.

Question: Do you think racial segregation hurts a region economically?

Answer: I certainly do. The damage may have been difficult to detect, as long as Negroes accepted the system stoically. But they no longer do this. We have reached the point of no return. Now a state such as North Carolina, which adjusts realistically to changing social patterns and makes a real effort to correct inequities in justice and opportunities, invariably takes the lead in industrial growth.

Question: Why do Negroes want to mix with whites? Cardinals do not mix with wrens, nor blackbirds with bluejays! Cattle do not mix with deer!

Answer: My *deer* sir: You racist bird watchers miss the point. We are trying to deal with problems related primarily to sociology, economics, and ethics, not ornithology.

Question: Why are you always talking about desegregation being the law of the land? The 1954 Supreme Court decision is *not* the law of the land. The Supreme Court does not make laws, Congress makes the laws. And Congress has made no laws to integrate.

Answer: The Supreme Court interprets the law, and the Constitution is the law. Whether the Fourteenth Amendment was forced upon the South and adopted through chicanery is a moot question, as it has been on the books for a good long time. What the racist should do, if he wants the situation changed, is to work for an amendment to the Constitution which would say that Negroes are *not* American citizens and are *not* entitled to equal treatment and equal justice.

Question: Why couldn't the segregationists have made the needed social changes and economic adjustments to give Negroes an even break *before* they gave up hope and resorted to the streets? Couldn't the racists see the handwriting on the wall?

Answer: Unfortunately, throughout history, those having an unfair advantage have seldom given up without a struggle, even though it would usually have been in their best interest to do so.

If this were not true there might have been no Reformation,

as there would have been no abuses in the Church to precip-
itate the schism.

There might have been no communism if the Russian
peasants had been exploited just a little bit less.

There might have been no labor unions if factory owners
at the turn of the century had been just a little more interested
in human rights.

There might have been no French Revolution if the French
leaders had been just a little more concerned about the plight
of the people. As to the Revolution, Marie Antoinette
thought the whole affair a big joke, and when she was told
that the people had no bread, she came up with a hilarious
retort that would put some of our present-day racist jokers to
shame. She said, "Let them eat cake." But Louis XIV was
more realistic about it and laid it right on the line—"After
us the deluge."

I wondered, as I read accounts of Police Commissioner
"Bull" Connor's activities in the spring of 1963, if he might
not have made a similar remark to Birmingham's former
mayor.

Question: Don't you think preachers should concentrate
on preaching the gospel and keep their noses out of social
problems?

Answer: I think social problems and men's treatment of
other men is part of the gospel; not the most important part,
but a very important part and one that should certainly rate a
mention now and then.

Question: Don't you think the best thing to do would be
to leave the solving of these social problems to the Lord?

Answer: This idea of dumping all of our troublesome problems on God has never seemed to me a likely way of winning
favor. When people advance this argument I am reminded of
the oft-repeated Southern Baptist story about a farmer who
had taken an especially sorry-looking piece of land and trans-
formed it into a prosperous-looking farm—the showplace

of the community. A neighbor remarked, "You and the Lord sure did a fine job with that piece of land." Replied the farmer, "Mebbe so, but you should have seen it when the Lord had it by himself!"

Question: Don't you think it is the Jews who are behind all of this racial agitation?

Answer: The racist has just got to find some one to blame for the changing social patterns, just anyone other than the Negroes themselves. As for the Jews, the ones I have known couldn't have been nicer. Instead of being able to say, "Some of my best friends are Jews," I can honestly say, "All of the Jews I know have been good friends to me." I just wish that more of my Christian friends had shown as much inclination to obey the second great commandment of the Christ they profess to follow as the Jews I have known have shown, even though they do not make the same profession of faith.

Question: Don't you think the Negroes are hurting their own cause by all of these demonstrations?

Answer: It is usually the people who would be very happy if the Negro's cause were hurt who ask this question. I think if they thought demonstrations really hurt the Negro's cause, they would secretly hope for more demonstrations (and maybe they do).

I suppose street demonstrations could reach such proportions that they would adversely affect the Negro's battle. I hope that this does not happen. I wish no demonstrations had been necessary; I do not think they are wanted by very many people of either race.

Question: Do you think we will ever be able to eliminate prejudice?

Answer: Of course not. If worst comes to worst and there is no one else to be prejudiced against, men will probably wind up being prejudiced against women, even though some of their best friends are women. All we are trying to do is to stop translating private prejudices into public policy.

Question: Why do you associate with so many segregationists?

Answer: I just associate socially with those I happen to like. I figure I can make allowances for what I think is their idiosyncrasy, as long as they make allowances for what they think is mine.

Question: Why are you people always talking about the "party of Lincoln" when urging Republicans to press for civil rights? Don't you know that Lincoln said in a speech, September 18, 1858, that he was not in favor of social and political equality for the white and Negro races?

Answer: This one has been pretty nearly worn out by writers of letters to the editors. As I get it, Lincoln said a lot of things (mostly things giving comfort to integrationists). But I wouldn't know about this as I was not around to listen. Liberals writing letters to editors tell the oft-repeated story about Robert E. Lee welcoming a Negro parishioner to partake of communion in his church, although Lee's fellow church members were not at all happy about the development. But, as the fellow says, "What has all of this got to do with the price of eggs?"

Question: How about all the race trouble in Chicago (or New York or Philadelphia or Washington, etc., etc.)? If everything is so nice for Negroes there, why all the trouble?

Answer: Chicago was a pretty tough town, even before there were more than a handful of Negroes on hand. The influx of five or six hundred thousand untrained, uneducated, and unemployed Negroes would hardly be likely to turn this asphalt jungle into a tranquil Monroe, Iowa. Nonetheless, there are a lot of good people of both races in Chicago who are attempting to cure the social and economic ills that seem to affect most large cities.

Question: In regard to the various civil-rights laws, it is not a question of civil rights with me, but rather of property rights. What right does the government have to tell the owner of a business whom he must serve and in this way interfere with the operation of the man's own business?

Answer: I have the feeling that the people who seem to worry so much about a man's right to operate his business "as he sees fit" have not once raised an objection to the various Jim Crow laws that have been on the statute books in several states for sixty or seventy years. These laws certainly told a man how he must run his business, because they told him he *must* segregate whether he wanted to or not. Obviously, it all depends upon whose ox is being gored.

Question: The young Negroes seem very intent upon eliminating racial barriers, but do you think they are supported by their elders?

Answer: Gordon Parks, fifty-year-old Negro author and staff photographer for *Life* magazine, wrote: "Our young people tell us boldly: We will not go on suffering while the white man insists on slow surrender through the law and time. If some speak to them of new laws and legislation, they answer: It's one thing to make a law and another thing to enforce it. If some speak to them of well-intentioned whites, they answer: If they are sincere, they will raise their voices above those of the racists. And if some tell them times are changing, they answer: WE are changing the TIMES. So my generation yields to them—and in doing so finds pride."[1]

Question: I have read in the newspapers about instances of racial discrimination in various foreign countries. What business do these foreigners have criticizing us for our policies? Aren't they just as bad?

Answer: Negro author Gordon Parks has traveled around the world and visited many countries. He writes: "Yes, I have learned. And after all the distance I've come, after all the dis-

[1] *Life* magazine, August 16, 1963.

tance I've been, I can say that the only place where I have
been excluded because of color from a hotel, restaurant,
church or movie is right here at home."[1]

Question: Why doesn't the Negro of today take the attitude of Booker T. Washington?

Answer: Booker T. Washington was a realist and probably
got for the Negro of his day all that it was possible to get. If
he were alive today he would probably be doing about what
Martin Luther King is doing.

I feel sure that Booker T. Washington would have been
deeply grieved had he realized he would some day become
the darling of the racists. During the Birmingham demonstrations a Negro mother appeared before a judge to plead for
her fifteen-year-old son who had been arrested. The judge
asked the woman what she thought of Booker T. Washington
and she answered, "I think he was a fine man in his day, but
his day is past. These young people won't take what we took."

Question: Isn't it true that integration "just won't work"
and hasn't worked any place it's been tried?

Answer: This is a common assertion made frequently by
the die-hard segregationists and restated frequently by politicians trying to please their constituents.

Well, I just don't know what these people are talking about
because, as a matter of fact, integration has worked well
wherever it has been tried and whenever a real effort has been
made to make it work. It has worked well for the Los Angeles
Dodgers and for every other professional baseball, football,
and basketball team and for the American Olympic teams. It
worked well for Loyola University's highly integrated basketball team as they knocked Mississippi State out of the national tournament in 1963, then went on to win the championship. (Too bad Mississippi's politicians can't take the
attitude of State's coach, Babe McCarthy, who said to report-
ers, "Let's talk about the way they play ball, not about the

[1] *Life* magazine, August 16, 1963.

color of their skin.") It worked well for the Arkansas Travelers baseball teams, whose leading hitter, a Negro, led the league in home runs.

It works well in Mitch Miller's TV show, in many other TV shows, in movies, in plays, and in the opera. It works well in factories which hold government contracts. It has worked well in public schools in Topeka, Kansas, Fayetteville, Arkansas, Omaha, Nebraska, Sioux City, Iowa, and thousands of other towns and cities that never made a headline.

It works well in Billy Graham's evangelistic meetings.

It seems to work just fine in nearly all our institutions of higher learning.

It will work whenever the people involved are not afraid of the competition and whenever they are big enough to grant to others the same rights and opportunities they want for themselves.

Question: Negroes are always talking about second-class citizenship. If they are second-class it is their own fault. Don't you think that if Negroes would just concentrate on improving themselves, and go to work they would be accepted as first-class citizens?

Answer: No American citizen should be penalized just because he is a member of a group which does not measure up to the standards of the average American in one way or another. The best way I can explain what I am trying to say is to tell about a trip I took through Mississippi. The thing about Mississippi that really impressed me was how much the state reminded me of Iowa. If anything, the soil in Mississippi looked even blacker and richer than that in Iowa. Mississippi obviously has all the natural resources Iowa has, and in addition to this, the people in Mississippi do not have to expend all of their time, energies, and money each winter trying to dig out from under the snow.

But in spite of all of the breaks given them by nature,

Mississippians rank at the bottom, or near the bottom, in just about everything good in America that is measured statistically. This includes rate of literacy, level of education, money spent per pupil on education, average hourly wage, and per capita income. Iowa ranks at the top, or near the top, in all of these same things.

Well, one might ask, why don't the people in Mississippi just "go to work"? Surely this would solve everything. But the white Mississippian will tell you that there are some very good reasons for the bad statistics. He will say that he has been discriminated against, and misunderstood by other Americans, that he is the victim of unjust laws, police brutality (by federal marshals), unequal charges (freight rates), and a multitude of other injustices. These are about the same things, of course, which Negroes also resent. But in the case of the Negro, they haven't had the advantage of having their boys holding down important committee chairmanships in the Congress.

Although I think by now my point has been made clear, I want to say that I would not want to see a fellow American segregated and discriminated against, just because he happened also to be a Mississippian.

People should be judged as individuals, according to their merits. And in addition to all that has been said, I'd hate to see the above-mentioned discrimination practiced, because I have some very good friends from Mississippi.

Question: Don't you think Negroes are inferior from an intelligence standpoint?

Answer: I don't think they are inherently inferior. You can find statistics to prove either side of this argument, depending upon whose literature you read. Since there is no such thing as a "culture-free" IQ test, conclusive proof is impossible to obtain. But I think it significant that well-educated and presumably intelligent white people are much less likely to worry about this than the fellow who dropped out in the tenth grade. This is one argument you cannot win. Neither can the segregationist. But if it is so all-fired important to him to feel sure that he is smarter than "any nigger," why, let him! The Negroes have their troubles, for sure, but this bird really has trouble and doesn't realize it.

The important thing about all of this is that we will never know, until the Negro finally gets an even break in education, and economically. When he does, if it turns out he really is inferior, he will just wind up on a lower-rated job, as any man would. But if it develops that he is just as capable and just as intelligent and has been held back solely because of his race for the past three or four hundred years in America, then a lot of people have a lot of guilt and a lot of sins to account for.

Question: Isn't there a high degree of immorality among Negroes?

Answer: If there is, there have certainly been contributing factors. One that comes readily to mind can best be explained by telling something that happened in my old home town in Iowa during the Great Depression. A good many people had to have help, but there was one family particularly hard on the county welfare funds. They had produced ten children, more or less, some in, some out, of wedlock. The welfare worker thought that the least they could do was to co-operate a little, and practice a little restraint—in view of the constant drain being made on the department's funds. But the man and the woman were both less than receptive to the idea. The husband said, "Durn it, the radio's busted, they ain't no gas for the car, we got no money for the picture show, and they just ain't nothing else to do!"

What is moral? The Bible says, Matthew 5:28: "Whosoever looketh on a woman to lust after her hath committed adultery with her already in his heart." The Bible also suggests that he who is without sin should cast the first stone.

Now who wants to step up and pitch the first rock? You'll

have to excuse me, please. I have to go and see a man about a dog.

Question: Isn't there a larger incidence of disease among Negroes?

Answer: There probably is, just as there is among any group economically handicapped. Therefore, I concentrate on the fair employment aspect of civil rights. I will say that while watching the telecast of the 1960 Olympic games, I got the impression Negroes were a pretty healthy lot. I also know quite a few of the colored kids in the Little Rock schools, and they all seem pretty healthy.

Question: Aren't Negroes lazy?

Answer: I have seen Negroes who appeared to be less than energetic. When I was a janitor, one of my first jobs with the railroad, I know I was not lazy. I was a real ball of fire. So it's hard to understand why Negro janitors push their brooms so slowly. Except, maybe, they feel as I would have. Had I realized that I'd never get a better job, I think I'd have shoved all the dirt under the stove when the boss wasn't looking even more often than I did. I might even have tossed the mop right through the window.

Question: Isn't it true that Negroes are inclined to be dishonest?

Answer: No doubt there have been instances of dishonesty. A segregationist friend and I were talking about this matter. He insisted he wasn't too critical when Negro maids took canned goods home (although, he said, you'd think after paying them fifty cents an hour they'd be more appreciative). But the thing he noticed was their lack of initiative. "You never hear of one getting out and selling a few thousand non-existent grain storage bins" was the clincher.

Question: Negroes don't really want integration, do they?

Answer: The Negroes I know want it. At least they don't want to be segregated. They want the same opportunities everyone else has. I don't know if the people who talk about

Negroes not wanting integration really believe it or are just trying to kid someone. The best answer to this question might be to ask yourself why Mississippi, where they say their "Nigras" are so happy they are nearly hysterical, doesn't lift the voting restrictions. Of course, they will insist (and with a straight face) that Negroes are not denied the vote. But the point is, they could actively encourage their "Nigras" to vote, and since the "Nigras" are all so enthusiastic about segregation, they would surely vote for the champions of segregation and give them even larger majorities than they have received in the past. Racists do a lot of talking about the dangers of the Negroes' "Block Vote"—BLOCK VOTING FOR WHAT?

Question: Don't you think the Negroes would be satisfied if they were not being stirred up by "agitators"?

Answer: They might be quiet. They would not be satisfied. Agitation is defined as commotion, excitement, trepidation, turmoil. Negroes have, at least until 1963, filed lawsuits, sat peacefully at lunch counters, or on buses. They have participated in group prayers and joined political action groups. Racists have formed mobs, thrown dynamite and "Molotov cocktails," shot through windows, burned churches, written all sorts of inflammatory literature.

Who's been doing the agitating?

Question: Aren't people in the North hypocritical about integration?

Answer: Many are. This does not mean that there are not a good many sincere people in the North, just as there are in the South, working to eliminate the effects of prejudice.

Question: Aren't the northern politicians who talk about civil rights just catering to the Negro vote?

Answer: Sometimes. And look out when the Negro vote starts to make itself felt in the South. But to be realistic about this question we should remember that in none of the big northern states do Negroes make up over 10 per cent of the population. It isn't the Negroes who elect the liberal senators and governors. These politicians would be unlikely to worry about what Negroes want if their white constituents wanted something else.

There are politicians, both North and South, who are sincere in their efforts to promote equal rights for Negroes.

Question: Most of the Negroes don't want integration and are not ready for it. They would not be able to compete successfully for jobs even if there were no discrimination. I think that when segregation is made illegal everywhere in the country, there will still be very few Negroes forcing themselves in "where they are not wanted," at white churches, schools, restaurants, and hotels. Don't you agree?

Answer: Then what are you worrying about?

Question: Don't you agree that you cannot force social changes?

Answer: You can't *make* a man do anything. Sometimes you can make him wish he had. Of course, you cannot eliminate robbery, murder, graft, or prostitution by laws or court orders. But you can certainly make these endeavors less appealing. One of the most frequently used arguments of the racist is that these Supreme Court decisions have "set our good race relations back one hundred years." This being the case, they must have been set back by several thousands of years by this time.

Others will tell you, "They might have integrated this school if they'd gone about it differently." I feel sure that if these people really thought the court decisions had slowed down integration, they'd be tickled pink, because if there is anything they want to do, it's to slow it down, or, preferably, stop it.

Actually, one breakthrough for the Negro usually seems to create another. And when the headlines appear, and there is trouble, police brutality, or cursing and jeering, a lot of white people feel the twinge of conscience and more and more Negroes say, "Why should I stand back and let the kids do it all?"

As to "setting back race relations," there may not be quite as much laughing and thigh-slapping by Willie, as he laughs at Mist' Charley's jokes. But if Willie gets that good job at the aircraft plant, he's really not going to worry much about what Mist' Charley thinks, as he has known all along how Mist' Charley really felt about him.

Question: Why do these agitators insist on tampering with our traditions and our way of life?

Answer: The only tradition the racist gives two hoots about is the tradition of keeping his foot on the Negro's neck. As to the way of life, the segregationist will be surprised to find that nothing has really changed, even after the Negro gets equal justice under the law. Industry is what is changing the way of life, not integration. And nobody is knocking industry. Our society has undergone constant change for as long as we've had any record. The change is certainly not going to stop happening now. The trend is not going to be reversed. Margaret Mitchell knew thirty years ago that the plantation economy was a civilization "gone with the wind." A constantly shrinking minority doesn't realize this yet.

Question: Don't you think the communists stir up racial troubles?

Answer: If they don't, I'm sure they would like to. But I don't understand why it never occurs to the people who talk so much about communists fomenting trouble, that they could make the communists very unhappy if they'd just help eliminate the cause of the trouble—failure to practice what we preach!

We should always remember that the struggle for a better life is a natural human tendency. Why should we give the communists credit for inspiring Negroes to claim their basic rights? The fact of the matter is that racists who join mobs, destroy property, make anonymous telephone calls, and raise hell in general, because of the Negro's efforts, are acting a good deal more like Stalin's secret police, or Hitler's Gestapo, than any of the people who urge equal opportunity for all citizens.

In the days of Oliver Cromwell, anyone in England who didn't agree was called a Papist, and in France he was called a Jacobin. In modern America, if he wants collective bargaining, TVA, a guaranteed annual wage or equal rights for all citizens, he is automatically called a Red by the "fright peddlers." In the past, in other lands, this gambit has worked. It won't work here because the tradition of freedom and the tradition of the worth of the individual run too deep. The unfortunate part about the fright peddlers' harangues is that people have heard the cry "Wolf, wolf," so long and so often that some of these days the real wolf might come around and gobble us up before we know what's happening.

It's a despicable thing to try and couple the best and noblest efforts of man (to rise from bondage, and to feel a real part of this great land) to something subversive.

Question: Don't Negroes have an offensive body odor?

Answer: Yes, if they don't bathe regularly. Don't we all?

Question: Isn't it true that Negroes have been unable to raise themselves to the position, economically, of the white man?

Answer: True. And until we start employing on the basis of merit and ability, we will never know if this is something inherent, or just a simple case of not being able to buy many shares of AT&T on your "cotton pickin'" wages. I heard all of these same arguments thirty years ago in connection with sports. They said that Negroes would never be able to compete successfully. And nobody could deny this, because it had never been tried. Maybe we need a Branch Rickey in industry!

Question: Aren't Negroes' brains smaller than the brains of white people?

Answer: Scientists say that they are, very slightly, by about the same degree that Eskimo's brains are larger than those of Caucasians. Scientists also say that the size of the brain has nothing to do with intelligence, but the Eskimos probably do not believe this. And this may account for the rumor that Eskimos are always going about saying that they don't mind a Caucasian as long as he stays in his place.

Question: Is it true that Negroes are superior to white people physically?

Answer: Not in any way, if my memory serves me correctly, and as I recall the sharing of shower rooms with colored athletes during my basketball-playing days.

Question: Don't Negroes have exceptional sexual capabilities?

Answer: When I asked a friend about this, he said he doubted it, but that he didn't know—that his opinion might be biased by his own conceit.

Question: Don't you think newspapers have been partly to blame for our racial troubles. Haven't they distorted the news?

Answer: All I know about this is in connection with the troubles in Little Rock. I saw this first hand, and thought the newspaper coverage quite accurate. Newspapers may sensationalize and exaggerate. But news is news. And this is what hurts. If there had been no unruly mobs, no inflammatory speeches, no threats to defy our government, and a little more counsel for good citizenship and Christian ethics at Little Rock, at Oxford, and at Birmingham, there would have been no news. There was mighty little news when Atlanta's schools were integrated, and when Clemson College enrolled Harvey Gnatt.

Question: I don't try to force my way into no country club. Why do "niggers" try to force themselves in "where they are not wanted"?

Answer: It is most unlikely that the fellow who asks this

question would, in fact, be found in "no country club." The more likely locale would be Joe's pool hall. And since he would be even less likely to be found reading this, my answer may well be a waste of time. But my explanation has been something like this: There is a great difference between a privately operated club and a place catering to the general public. The country club is trying to give its members exactly what the fellow asking the question wants—a little prestige. But the country club is private, and if they won't let you in, you can tell yourself, and everyone else, that you didn't want in their durned club anyways—you'd rather join the Elks.

Yes, a person can insult and humiliate another person, if he wishes, within certain bounds. It's a free country. But when your church does it to you, when your town, your state, or your nation does it to you, it's a pretty low blow.

Question: Don't you think integration will result in a great many racially mixed marriages?

Answer: No. I have lived in northern cities where Negroes, although discriminated against in many ways, were still pretty well integrated in schools and other public places. Interracial marriages were extremely rare. It seems obvious that in a region where feeling runs high on the subject, racially mixed marriages would be even more infrequent.

Racists do a lot of talking about being "forced to mix." But a good friend, a former segregationist, did not seem to be worried. He told me he had decided to quit worrying about integration. He said he managed to segregate himself from the white people he didn't want to be around and felt sure he could do the same with Negroes. But he also said that he had some good colored friends, and that if he met one of them down town and felt like going into a lunch counter to drink a cup of coffee with his friend, he would like to be able to do so without feeling that he had committed a crime. My friend also confided that he had come to the conclusion there would never be a law passed requiring a person to marry someone he did not wish to marry—except for obvious reasons.

Certain racial or religious groups have managed to marry pretty well within their own groups. There was the Jewish fellow in a Deep South state and a segregationist warned him that if the schools were integrated his daughter might wind up marrying a Negro. The answer was, "Listen, mister, my daughter is not going to marry *any* gentile!"

Question: Would you want your daughter to marry a Negro?

Answer: This question is never asked in good faith. It is about like the question, "Have you stopped beating your wife? Answer yes or no."

The question is asked because the questioner knows you cannot win. You cannot answer with a yes or no about your wife; or at least that would be my situation. You have to say, "I never did beat my wife, so how can I stop?" In the case of "old faithful," the "Would you want your daughter" routine, if you say yes, then they will tell you you are out to mongrelize (whatever that means) the race. If you say no, then you are obviously a hypocrite.

It would be nice to counter this question with another question: "Which Negro?", as I am sure there are many Negro young men more honest, kind, intelligent, and sincere than some of the white men your daughter might get stuck with. But it is not that simple. You would probably have to say no to the question because our society at present would not let such a marriage succeed. This would also be true, to a lesser degree, in talking about marriages between Caucasians and Orientals, and between people of differing religious faiths. But this reasoning does not apply in other areas. Our society is about ready to grant Negroes the citizenship rights of equal justice and opportunity that should have been theirs in the first place.

Question: Why do you get so worked up over the Negroes' troubles. It's their problem. Let them solve it.

Answer: It's everybody's problem. We all know the arguments usually used to the effect that you can't keep a man down in the ditch without getting down there with him. But with me it's more than this. The whole business of race-caste does something to my pride, even though I am a member of the privileged group. I do not like to get preferential treatment I did not earn—an automatic advantage I neither want nor need. If you think that you need it, or must have it, then I can see your point.

Question: Don't you think Negroes should "stay in their place"? Or, I don't mind a "nigger," if he stays in his place. Or, the "niggers" in this town "know their place."

Answer: I have found that the most effective way to combat this timeworn cliché is to demand a definition of the place referred to.

There are many questions which can be asked, such as, where is this place? Is it geographic or psychic? Is it mental or physical? Would *you* want to be confined to this *place?* Is it a nice place? Are any people besides Negroes confined to this place?

Nothing stops the questioner as quick as the request for a definition. I find that segregationists just naturally suppose that everyone knows about this "place," yet when pressed for an explanation of it, the segregationists appear utterly confounded. But since it is mentioned so often, I feel the matter merits a thorough study, even though we cannot get the answers from the segregationists.

If it is a place characterized by a humble origin and by economic handicaps, then it must be only for Negroes, since we applaud white people who indignantly refuse to stay in such a place. We are familiar with the Horatio Alger stories of the poor immigrant boys who came to our shores with only a few pennies in their pockets but rose to positions of great wealth or prominence. All of this is supposed to be in the American tradition. So it must be just black Americans who are expected to remain in this "place."

I usually fall back upon the definition my son and I gave in our book *This Is What We Found* (page 33): "This frequently mentioned place has never been clearly defined, but it seems to us it is really a supposedly escape-proof psychic and economic prison. Escape has been difficult, but a surprising number of Negroes have managed it; and the number is growing rapidly."

Question: How about Washington, D.C.?

Answer: I'll swear I don't know what the racists would do if it were not for Washington, D.C. Segregationist writers of letters to the editor would be hard pressed indeed if they could not "view with alarm the terrible conditions." Maybe we liberals should not begrudge these people the small pleasure they can get from talking about Washington, because their pleasures have been few in recent years. But in talking to those with real concern, we can point out that Washington, among the country's twenty-five largest cities, does not rank first in crime, but thirteenth—about halfway down the list, or par for the course! This may not be much consolation for someone who may have taken a tap on the noggin while walking the streets of our nation's capital. But we must remember that Washington is unique in that its people are not permitted to govern themselves. Segregationist-minded congressmen with a lot of seniority have seen to that.

Louisville, Kentucky, is a city that governs itself. It has a Negro population about like Little Rock's, percentage-wise. Louisville was one of the first cities in a border or mid-South state to desegregate its schools. It did so with no trouble.

A news item in June 1963 read as follows:

LOUISVILLE SETS PACE FOR DIXIE
WITH ITS FAST INTEGRATION MOVES

Louisville, Ky.—This border city, with its heavy southern exposure, has been setting an admirable example in good race relations that other southern cities could beneficially follow.

Some visitors to rapidly changing Louisville, seeing Negroes in leading hotel lobbies, sitting anywhere in buses, going to any movie houses, and being greeted by a Negro receptionist at the Mayor's office, have been heard to remark that Louisville is showing many aspects of a Northern city.

What the city government has been trying to do over the past few years is to head off trouble before it begins—guided by the rule that an ounce of prevention is better than a pound of cure.

MAKING PROGRESS

The obvious result can be seen in the fact that Louisville is making more effective and practical progress in race relations betterment than any other city in the South. And this progress has resulted in gaining the confidence and trust of Louisville Negroes.

All of the city's schools, parks, swimming pools, restaurants and theaters have been desegregated during the past eight years without much fan-fare and without any serious incidents.

The latest step in the city's march towards desegregation was passage of an ordinance banning discrimination in barbershops, bowling alleys and all other places of public accommodations.

The ordinance carries fines of $100 for violation, and the Board of Aldermen passed it two days after violence reached its peak in Birmingham.

The city's Mayor William O. Cowger has been showing admirable leadership in race relations activities in the city. He backed the ordinance, which had been sponsored by the city's Human Relations Commission.

The commission is an integrated body with 11 associated committees with a total membership of 180, of which 45 are Negroes.

EXTENDED PROGRESS

The new city ordinance did not mark the beginning of progress, but only extended progress that had been made over the past few years. As an example, a survey made by the Human Relations Commission revealed that 268 of the city's 410 restaurants already integrated before passage of the ordinance.

Most of these lowered racial barriers following mass demonstrations by Negro students two years ago.

Following passage of the new anti-discrimination ordinance, Lyman T. Johnson, president of the Louisville NAACP, issued a statement commending the Board of Aldermen. He added:

"We look forward now to further advances toward full employment, housing and training opportunity for all our citizens regardless of race."

Charles Steele, director of the Urban League, also lauded the ordinance as representing steady progress in the city's racial relations. But he reminded:

"This is no time to sit down, look back and say, 'See, look what we have done.' Move on. The next thing is segregated housing. We are already working on the problem."

Much of the credit for the city's steady progress and improvement in race relations can be attributed to effective leadership, traditional moderation and good communication between whites and Negroes.

Also, Louisville's Negroes have long been well organized politically and have favored direct action. Mass demonstrations and a shopping boycott two years ago brought quick results.

"This woke us up," remarked one important white citizen. "Those demonstrations got us moving when we had relaxed after integration of our schools. We don't want to see any more demonstrations."

DIRECT NEGOTIATIONS

Louisville's racial problems are now being dealt with through direct negotiations and the Human Relations Commission's committees. Effective and quick work by the commission has served to ward off new demonstrations.

"This should not be taken to mean that we are merely trying to keep the peace," said J. Mansir Tydings, executive director of the Commission. "What we are trying to do is to continue to make progress in human relations."[2]

Considering the progress which has been made in Louisville, and in the entire state of Kentucky for that matter, we have to conclude that Kentucky has just about had her "fire next time," and is about ready to forget about racial problems and get back to such things as thoroughbred horses, UK basketball, and the Kentucky Derby.

So when people say to me, "Look at Washington. Would you want Little Rock to be like Washington?" I say, "Look at Louisville." I can also tell them about other Louisvilles all over America, some of which I have known personally.

Question: I have heard that the post office in Dallas promoted three Negroes "around" about fifty white people who were more qualified. Isn't this discrimination?

Answer: Your desire to help eliminate discrimination is heart-warming.

[2] Chicago *Daily Defender.*

Question: Negroes are always complaining about being discriminated against economically. But I read an article about a Negro who started out penniless and with only a sixth-grade education who wound up as a millionaire and owner of a large factory. Doesn't this prove that Negroes can get ahead, if they really try?

Answer: Individuals, white or Negro, sometimes have sufficient business acumen or sales ability to achieve great success by going into business for themselves. This is a talent you either do or do not have. People who do have it are likely to assume, human nature being what it is, a look-what-I-did attitude. Most of us are not blessed with such talent. I am afraid I would have a difficult time selling a life jacket to a drowning man. So I have had to make my living by working for someone else. This is the manner in which the vast majority of all people manage to have an income upon which to pay taxes. And this is where the discrimination comes in. If I had possessed sufficient talent, intelligence, and drive it would have been possible for me to wind up as president of a railroad. At least I would not have been held back because of my race. I started my career on the railroad as a track laborer, and there was nothing to hinder me from taking the many intermediate steps from there to the presidency. Had I been black I would not have been permitted to take these intermediate steps regardless of my talent, intelligence, and drive. And I am talking about an industry that has been one of the best about providing employment, at good wages for Negroes.

Question: Don't you think "these Negro leaders," who keep the Negroes stirred up, are just doing it for personal gain and for the money they can get out of it?

Answer: I have no way of knowing what the "real" motives of anyone are—except myself, and I am not 100 per cent sure about that. My guess is that most of the Negro leaders are very sincere and dedicated to the cause of obtaining equal human rights. Questioning the motives of leaders is a commonly used device of those who would divide and conquer. Almost identical accusations have been made for years, often by the same people, against labor leaders. I am more familiar with, and personally acquainted with labor leaders, than I am with civil rights leaders. For several years while I was represented by a labor organization I generally felt that it was my duty to take the side of labor, when controversies arose. Now, representing management, I can see the other side of the issue quite clearly. But I am happy to say that the company I work for has a very enlightened policy in dealing with their employees, and has scrupulously abided by any and all agreements made between them and the various labor organizations which represent railroad employees. The property rights of the railroads have not taken precedence over human rights. But there is such a striking analogy between the growth, and difficulties, and the leaders of organized labor, and the growth, difficulties, and leaders of civil rights organizations, that when asked about it, I generally quote from page 47 of *This Is What We Found:* "To return to the progress made by the Negro through organized labor, we cannot help but notice many similarities and parallels between the efforts of the laboring man (regardless of color) to improve his position and the efforts of the Negro to improve his. With each group, any indication of a competent organization was violently opposed at first. In each case, the opposition could be depended upon to say, 'We were getting along just fine here until these outside agitators came in stirring up trouble.' 'Everything was nice and peaceful.' Or, 'We know what's best for our employees (or Nigras.)'"

It probably was peaceful. But in the case of the laborer he could be discharged without regard to length of service to make room for the boss's nephew; worked overtime without additional pay, his just grievances ignored and salary kept at levels lower than required for a decent standard of living. In the case of the Negro, it was also "peaceful," but Negro filling station attendants could be shot for arguing with white customers about the correct amount of change. They could be denied decent housing in the Chicago area and such places as Dearborn, Michigan, and denied Pullman accommodations and be restricted to substandard schooling during this era of peace.

In each case, it could be stated with truth that some organization leaders were more concerned about personal gain than with progress for the group they represented. Each group has, no doubt, made mistakes. In the opposition to each group, there have certainly been sincere men who were kind and good and motivated by high standards of morality, but the fact remains that no one knows the needs and desires of any group of people as well as members of that group. No one will represent them with more integrity than they represent themselves. Refusal or inability of any group to defend themselves, regardless of strenuous efforts to prevent this defense, only results in loss of respect for the group involved.

Members of the dominant (white) group who stoutly maintain that they are looking out for the best interests of the Negro, and that they will "take care" of him, are no more likely to do so than the company or "dummy" union is to represent fully the laboring man. The basic purpose of company unions is to blunt the effectiveness or the appeal of the bona fide union. A similar aim to blunt effectiveness is behind arguments we hear from some whites that they can do the best job of looking after the interests of the Negro.

In comparing the similarities between the difficulties encountered by organized labor and by organizations representing racial minority groups, we are confronted with one inescapable fact. Those areas of our country which have offered the strongest opposition to organized labor have also been most vehement in opposition to organizations representing racial minorities. They refuse to admit either group has any rights not given to them because of benevolence. Union labor is now beginning to be more fully accepted in these areas, but by constant appeal to race prejudice, the working man has been kept from realizing that he has been used in much the same way as has the Negro.

In recent years, we have observed that nearly all our large and successful corporations have been willing to meet with representatives of organized labor and work toward a solution of problems in good faith. Also, many of these corporations have followed practices that largely eliminated the need for bargaining.

It also seems obvious that, had the Negro not had many grievances in connection with double standards of justice, no organizations would have been formed to represent him. The Negro, like the rest of us, would prefer to be in a position where organization is not necessary.

Question: Doesn't the Bible teach that we should segregate Negroes?

Answer: Not by any stretch of the imagination. It does stress a strong common bond between all believers, and urges separation from "the world," or from unbelievers. So, if you are white and a dedicated Christian, you should prefer the company of a Negro Christian to the company of the white agnostic. Is not the bond of Christian brotherhood stronger than any other?

Question: Why do you constantly attack segregationists? Are you not being as intolerant of them as they are of Negroes?

Answer: You have me all wrong. Some of my best friends are segregationists.

Question: I think Negroes should have their civil rights,

but I think they are trying to move too fast right now, don't you?

Answer: I always answer this one with another question, namely, how fast would you consider "just right"?

It nearly always turns out that the segregationist's concept of "just right" is a speed of absolute zero.

Question: Why don't you "bleeding hearts" who worry so much about the Negro take a little interest in the plight of the American Indians? They are kept on their reservations and not even allowed to vote!

Answer: A generation ago I attended a college in Kansas, where a good many American Indians were enrolled. Somehow they had escaped from their reservations. Those over twenty managed to vote at the same time everyone else did. They participated fully in all school activities. One of our best athletes was an Indian. We did Indian dances at our pep rallies. I dated an Indian girl. The Indians there had the same chance to get a skilled job as the rest of us did (which at that time was practically no chance at all). So I did not realize, until reading all of the letters to the editor, in the *Arkansas Democrat,* how badly Indians were being treated.

Question: Don't you think that immediate and total integration of the schools in the South would create chaos in the educational system?

Answer: I don't know. It might. The Supreme Court had this in mind when they specified "deliberate speed." Nearly all southern educators involved have worked out plans to make the transition very gradual. Negro groups have indicated, or at least they did for a long time, that all they wanted was a real display of good faith in setting up plans for desegregation. But it is these same educators, such as former Little Rock Superintendent Virgil Blossom, who tried to make the process as gradual as possible, who literally caught hell from the segregationists.

Question: How will it all be settled?

Answer: Well, there is no doubt that the race issue is one of the most vexing problems of our times. Finding a solution is surely important. The trouble is that solutions suggested by the segregationists and those advanced by integrationists are so far apart that there seems to be no middle ground. We are often confronted with equally difficult problems in other areas, such as foreign relations, labor-management, and in religious matters. I have heard the suggestion made, by people talking about alternatives to thermonuclear war, that it was just too bad we could not resolve our problems by staging a big football game or athletic contest of some sort between our country and Russia, for example, and be governed by the outcome of the contest rather than having to resort to annihilation. Maybe we could use the same approach to the race issue. We could have a big "tag team rassle" staged in Jackson, Mississippi's, new municipal stadium. To be perfectly fair and to keep everything separate but equal, we would have the same number (three) on each team. The team defending racial justice could be made up of Joe Louis, Jimmy Brown, and Roosevelt Brown. White supremacy's trio would consist of Ross Barnett, George Wallace, and Strom Thurmond. The late wrestler Gorgeous George's valet could appropriately spray each contestant before the match, for the benefit of their opponents. The results would be binding, best two out of three falls. Martin Luther King could act as referee, and Thurgood Marshall and Earl Warren as judges. All proceeds should be split evenly between the N.A.A.C.P. and the D.A.R.

Now wouldn't this beat trying to settle the issue "in the streets"?

Question: It isn't a matter of segregation with me, it's states' rights. The federal government is just getting too much power. I think racial discrimination is wrong, but I thought President Kennedy's civil rights program was just a scheme to get more power for the federal government, and President

Johnson is even worse. White people have civil rights, too, you know. Don't you agree?

Answer: Yes, I agree. But I have always asked the fellow who says it's all a matter of "states' rights" just how the various desegregation moves and the "centralized government" have abridged *his* rights. I always had the feeling that as far as President Kennedy was concerned, the Kennedy haters were the same old bunch who disliked Negroes, labor unions, or Catholics, either separately or as a combination. I have a friend who did a lot of talking about how President Kennedy was leading us down the road to ruin. He insists he is for equal rights for Negroes, but that he can't stand the fiscal policies of the present administration. He thinks the only difference between President Johnson and President Kennedy is that President Johnson may get a little "tougher," and therefore be a little more effective in getting legislation passed. He thinks the deficit spending of our past five presidents has ruined us, and that we should do away with the income tax. In fact he says his taxes are now so high that he has difficulty making the payments on his split-level home, his three cars, his motorboat, his deep freeze, his central air conditioning, his houseful of new furniture, and his stereo!

Question: How about the trouble in the Congo? Isn't this proof of the Negroes' barbarism?

Answer: It gets a trifle wearisome trying to do something constructive in race relations, while having to listen continuously to stories about conditions in the Congo, or in other parts of the world. After all, we do not discriminate against Americans of Russian descent because the country of their ancestors is atheistic. But we hear this Congo matter mentioned so frequently it is best to be ready for the racist.

You will notice that when a racist talks about Africa he invariably mentions the Congo. He seldom mentions Nigeria.

When the Belgians got to the Congo a good many years ago the people there were operating very few steel mills and their parliamentary machinery was a trifle crude. In fact, if these people could just beat the heat, the yaws, and leprosy, and outrun the tsetse fly, they thought they had it made. When the Belgians left, in 1960, conditions hadn't changed a great deal because the Belgians seemed to want it that way.

Now the British on the other hand, (despite a slight tendency toward hanky-panky), are pretty good fellows. More to the point, they are realists.

Twenty African nations preceded Nigeria to independence[3] but Nigeria emerged not only as a giant in population, but in stature as well. Although the nation is composed of what were once 250 different tribal groups, with different cultures and language, it is one of the most stable and democratic of all the new nations.

Nigeria stands as a monument to the good side of colonialism. The people were well trained in the arts of parliamentary maneuvers. They were trained in industrial skills. In 1914 a Nigerian was chosen to serve on the advisory council in Lagos with the British and in 1922 a Nigerian was elected to the legislature.

After independence, Nigerian Prime Minister Abubakar Tafawa Balewa said, "We are grateful to the British whom we have known, first as masters, then as leaders, finally as partners, but always as friends."

Lagos, the capital of Nigeria, is a city of gleaming skyscrapers, air-conditioned motels, supermarkets, and department stores. Its streets are jammed with vehicular traffic and a new TV station is in operation.

In the Congo, when freedom was granted, there were not more than a handful of college-trained men in the entire country. But in Nigeria, there were hundreds. Today, there are five major universities in Nigeria and twenty-two hundred Nigerians graduate from universities each year.

[3] *Reader's Digest,* March 1963.

In a television speech ("Meet the Press") in the spring of 1963, Governor Wallace made the statement that Alabama was "no utopia."

Nigeria is no utopia either. There is corrupt politics there. There is vice there. There is poverty. They are far ahead of many countries in their standard of living, but still far behind many others. But they seem to be moving in the right direction. And for this reason the racists are not likely to tell you about Nigeria.

Question: Won't I lose all my friends if I speak out against racial discrimination?

Answer: This is a question that many white liberals have had to answer. Many of us in the South have had to face our "moment of truth" because of it.

It has been my experience that you need not lose your friends. However, it is important that you give the other fellow the same right to his opinion that you want for yourself. When with people who are strong segregationists you can easily find topics of conversation other than race. But at the same time, when your segregationist friends insist on pursuing the matter, you should leave no doubt in their minds. Let them know that you think racial discrimination and segregation are in conflict with Christian ethics and with the American creed.

In my particular case, I believe that my intense interest in the Negro's struggle actually made friends for me, even among moderate segregationists. I think what happened was that when I studied the Bible to find out what I could about its teachings on prejudice, I realized how much emphasis Christ placed on human relations. Then, to be consistent, I could hardly go out of my way to be kind, friendly, and generous to Negroes, and withhold these same things from white people—even segregationists.

You'd be surprised how people, regardless of their beliefs, reciprocate to honest gestures of friendship.

All this is not to say that there won't be those few who will stop being your friend because you do not agree with them. In our case there have been very few, but there have been some. I am sorry that these people stopped being my friends. I wish they had not done this, as I wanted their friendship, even though I did not agree with them. I hope the day will soon come when the issue is resolved and friendships will no longer be broken because of diverging views on racial prejudice.

Question: Why should *we* pay all the taxes so the Negroes can lie around and draw welfare checks and spend their money on whisky and new cars?

Answer: One of our big troubles is putting too much emphasis on the word "we," and too little on the word "us." The racist never wants to think of the Negro as a fellow citizen, as to do so would cause his whole set of arguments to collapse like a pack of cards.

Actually the people who really get gouged on taxes are likely to be liberal on the race issue. It is the people Mr. Faubus likes to refer to as the "good hard-working folks," who pay no more taxes than Negroes, in proportion to their incomes, who scream to high heaven about the high taxes they pay, upon which the Negroes are supposed to live like kings. These are the people who circulate crudely written and not very funny verses such as this one:

"THE WASHINGTON, D.C., NATIONAL ANTHEM."

Oh say can you see by de dawn's early light
How we gather by de creekbank waiting fo de fish to bite?
We is a bunch of niggers without a thought or care
We's done convinced de gov'ment dat we needs welfare.
We drives round in big ca'hs and we has chilluns by de score
Cause each one we brings pays us $25 more.
We is paid to vote, we is paid to sin

An de politicians keep de checks a comin' in.
De white folks works from sun to sun
Just to pay de taxes while us have all de fun.
We waits each month for dat slip wid de figgers
Dat's what we lives for — us lucky niggers.

Literary gems like these are invariably made available to
and by white people just a step up the cultural and economic
ladder from the kind of Negroes they talk about. The gram-
mar used in these verses usually leaves much to be desired,
but the appreciative reader usually manages to become hysterical at the dialect he and his forebears taught the Negro in the
first place.

I would not dignify what passes for humor with racists by
retelling it if it were not for the tragic fact that the thoughts
expressed reflect what many people really believe, or at least
try desperately to make themselves think they believe about
Negroes. Let us analyze the words of the verse carefully:

"Without a thought or care." This is about as far from the
truth as it is possible to get. The Negro spiritual "Nobody
Knows the Trouble I've Seen" is closer to the real picture.

"De white folks works from sun to sun." Because of the nature of my work I have been called to work at such hours as
four, five, and six o'clock in the morning. About the only people I saw on the streets at those hours were Negro men and
women waiting for buses, to go to work. The white folks, for
the most part, started showing up at 8 A.M.

"While us have all de fun." I have enjoyed water skiing on
Arkansas lakes for some time. Water skiing is fun, and the increased participation in this sport by so many people no
doubt reflects our increased affluency. In the summer of
1963 I saw my first Negro on water skis. The friends I was
with thought it was hilarious. They had no objection, but
simply had never seen a Negro enjoying himself in this manner before. "Us have all de fun"?

"We's done convinced the gov'ment dat we needs welfare."

You have to assume that the segregationists who complain about welfare grants to Negroes believe Negroes should go hungry if they are without funds and without jobs.

It is particularly ironical that these racists, who do all the talking about Negroes not working and living on welfare, are the very people who have done everything they possibly could to keep the Negro from getting an even economic break through decent, well-paid jobs. In other words, they have seen to it that the Negro wound up on the welfare rolls, then criticized him for being there.

Even so, the Negroes have done a lot of work in this country whenever they had the chance. In no industry is this more obvious than on the railroad. In the years I have lived in Little Rock I have become particularly conscious of the important part the American Negro has played in building the South, and particularly in building the railroads. They carried the timbers, drove the steel, shoveled the coal, and loaded the freight. They have been doing these things for a century or more, back to the time of the legendary John Henry. John Henry was reputed to be the strongest man alive and he worked with construction gangs driving railroad tunnels through southern mountains. Eventually automation, in the form of the steam drill, caught up with him. A contest was arranged between the man and machine and the strain on his heart was said to have caused John Henry's death. Work crews immortalized the fabled strong man with the ballad "Jawn Henry":

> "Jawn Henry said to de Capt'in:
> A man ain't nothin' but a man:
> If I let yore steam drill beat me down,
> I'll die with th' hammer in m' han'."

I have concluded that when it comes to love of the railroads and trains, color is irrelevant. Whenever crises have come, such as wrecks, fires, or floods, we have all worked to-

gether to get the trains rolling again and could say with John
Henry, "A man ain't nothin' but a man."

Question: What about these Negro women who have a
"whole raft" of illegitimate children just to get welfare payments?

Answer: Well, this, like sin, is something you just about
have to be against. But before we condemn an entire race of
people, most of whom have certainly been culturally and
economically handicapped, it might be well to take a look at
the morals of other peoples who have not been so handicapped.

People in the Scandinavian countries are known for their
broad-mindedness about premarital sex. The French have
never been noted for their restraint. Other Europeans from
whom many of our ancestors sprang have similar broad-
minded attitudes. But it took the peccadilloes of Christine
Keeler and her friends to bring these issues into sharp focus.
A friend and I were discussing a *Time* magazine article[4]
about Miss Keeler. I quote a few excerpts from the article
which was pretty much like related articles on the same subject, published in just about all of our magazines and newspapers: "There is a widespread feeling that Britain's moral
machinery is not grinding as harshly as it used to. Much in
English life today suggests decadence and dissolution. Since
the girls were driven off the streets four years ago they have
taken to advertising their services in shop windows as 'mas-
seuses,' 'models,' or 'French teachers.' London's booming
strip-tease parlors offer some of the crudest live pornography
to be seen publicly in Europe. Its parks in summer are pre-
empted by couples who aren't just necking. One third of all
teen-age brides in Britian are already pregnant. Innumerable
scandals preceding the Profumo case suggest considerable
promiscuity, along with sexual arrangements infinitely more

[4] *Time*, June 21, 1963.

complex than the old-fashioned triangle. Psychologist G. M. Carstairs commented recently: 'Popular morality is now a wasteland, littered with the debris of broken conventions. Concepts such as honor, or even honesty, have an old-fashioned sound, but nothing has taken their place.'

"This harsh judgment may overlook the fact that Britain was never the sort of place Victorian morality pretended it was.

"Says Malcolm Muggeridge: 'There's always been a lot of high-grade whoring in this country.' There is a lot of past evidence to prove him right. George IV had his queen tried publicly for infidelity; in the early 18th century, an Archbishop of York maintained a harem at his palace. The 18th century Christine Keeler was a Miss Chudleigh.

"One of the most successful of all high-society hustlers was Harriette Wilson, a Regency beauty whose guest register would have read like Burke's Peerage; when she started publishing her memoirs, she managed to collect double dividends from many former patrons who preferred not to be immortalized.

"Since the mid-19th century, sin for a politician has meant getting caught at it. At least three officially virtuous Prime Ministers, Lord Palmerston, Arthur Balfour and Lloyd George were inveterate adulterers."

After discussing this article with my friend, I suggested that if the British want to engage in the type of extracurricular activities mentioned, it is their business. But that if any of them, or their descendants show up here, segregationists, to be consistent, should insist on segregating them, and should deny them basic human rights.

Really, I hope it never comes to this. I don't think I could tolerate being segregated. You see, my ancestors were English. They came over on a boat—sometime between the *Mayflower* and the *Queen Mary*.

Question: Why do you worry so much about Negroes being

mistreated? If Negroes had the upper hand it would be the other way around. If you went over to the Congo they'd put you in a pot and boil you.

Answer in three parts:

1. They might eat me. I don't think they could stomach you!

2. Two wrongs do not make a right.

3. American Negroes are not Congolese. A few of them have ancestors who lived in the Congo, but a lot more of them are your relatives. And this is because there were a lot of segregationists a hundred years ago who weren't kidding when they said, "Some of my best friends are Negroes."

Question: Why don't you integrationists who are always talking about brotherly love practice what you preach, and integrate your churches?

Answer: No one would be unhappier than the fellow asking this question if you did what he suggested. But it's a good question, and I wish I had the answer. Negro comedian Dick Gregory said he would be welcomed at most bars in Chicago, but in very few churches. "Maybe," he opined, "they have the crosses on the wrong buildings!"

To be realistic about this, I suppose there would not be a great deal of integration in churches, because of residential patterns, even if Negroes were made to feel welcome. But I just cannot see barring anyone from any house of worship. I'll confess I have endured a good many sermons that were not greatly inspiring, and I envied the Negro who was not there. Surely, I thought, he was doing better where he was. But I have also heard sermons that offered something of value, and in such cases if a man wants to come and listen, I would welcome him.

Question: I don't mind sitting down and eating in a restaurant with a well-dressed, obviously cultured Negro. I don't mind seeing these people integrated in all of the public places. But a lot of Negroes are uncouth, dirty, smelly, and illiterate.

Don't you think they will take advantage of the situation and try to force themselves in where they are not wanted?

Answer: Some might. I suppose we could establish certain rules of conduct, dress, and education and make compliance with these rules mandatory. But we would have to apply the rules equally, and I wouldn't want them to get too finicky in their requirements, or I might be blackballed (or white-balled, if you prefer).

Question: Why don't you go back to where you came from, if you don't like it here?

Answer: But I do like it here. I think Arkansas is a fine state, with a great future, and is making good progress in elim-inating racial prejudice and discrimination. If you don't like it, and don't like the way things are going, why don't you leave?

Question: Since I originated in the North, I hesitate to speak out against prejudice. Wouldn't the people here make it unpleasant for me?

Answer: On the contrary, being from the North is an asset. The southern white liberal will welcome and appreciate your help as long as he thinks you are sincere. The southern white moderate, the realist, will welcome a little variety in ideas and admire a man willing to "think for himself." The racist will make allowances for you because he will figure you are a Damn Yankee anyway, and don't know any better.

Question: Don't you think that Negroes in the schools will drastically lower the standards of morals and education?

Answer: This is a frequently asked question. Racists cer-tainly seem greatly concerned about the morals and the ethics of the Negro children entering the previously all-white schools. The sensitivities of the people doing the complaining are easily offended. But permit me to quote from a printed card, which was originated and circulated by the very people doing the complaining:

NOTICE TO STUDENTS

LITTLE ROCK CONGO HIGH SCHOOL is not being niggerized fast enough to suit us.

Effective immediately, all boys may use the girls' restrooms, and girls may use boys' restrooms. Use whichever restroom is convenient.

YOU TRASHY BASTARDS have got to learn to do things THE NIGGER WAY.

SCHOOL BOARD

This card is typical of those circulated in the Little Rock schools during the early days of desegregation. You can see, after reading these profound words, what high cultural standards the extreme segregationist usually has. Personally, I'd hate to think that, even if I was trying to promote segregation, this was the best I could do.

Question: I notice that a lot of "do-gooders" who write in against segregation do not sign their names. Why are they so afraid to sign their names? Now I am a strong segregationist and am not afraid to sign my name! It is a sad state of affairs when a person is afraid to sign his name.

Answer: It is indeed.

Question: The Negroes have come a long way in this country and are a lot better off than people in other countries. Why can't they be satisfied?

Answer: I can't say for sure how Negroes feel about things that happened a hundred years ago. I know how I feel. I think that progress is interesting to read about, but I am more interested in making history than reading about it. What I am really interested in for my family, my friends, and myself is the way things are right now, or one year from now, or five years from now. If I thought I had been getting a raw deal I wouldn't stop trying to correct it, just because it was only half as raw as it used to be. In fact, evidence of progress would probably increase my zeal. I have a feeling that this is exactly the way the Negro looks at it.

Question: I believe in brotherhood but feel that I am the Negro's "older brother." Such being the case I naturally can not treat him as an equal.

Answer: This is a pretty silly argument and will get, deservedly, a silly answer. It is used frequently by religious people whose consciences bother them because of what the Bible has to say about various aspects of human relation.

I would say that older brothers are not necessarily smarter, kinder, or more just than younger brothers. Witness Cain and Abel. I would also say anyone would have a tough time keeping me away from a dime-store lunch counter, after letting an older brother of mine walk right up, sit down, and order a hamburger.

Question: Why are the Negroes always demanding equality? There is no such thing as equality. Different people have different abilities and you have to earn your first-class citizenship.

Answer: Some would question Khrushchev's classification as a "first-class" citizen. For that matter he is not a citizen of any kind—of America. But if he came here, I doubt if they would keep him out of the best hotel around, or even out of a dime-store lunch counter (maybe Disneyland) because he had not "earned" his first-class citizenship.

Actually, no one that I know says that all people are equal. All any civil-rights advocate is working for is equality of justice and opportunity.

When I was in college I was like the storied cricket who fiddled and sang all summer, and laid nothing by for the long winter ahead. I seldom glanced inside a textbook. Another fellow in the same house stayed in his room nightly until midnight or later, studying diligently, while I was out with other undergrads making merry. I think the studious fellow and I had about the same talent and brain power, but he is now head of the research and development department of a nationally known corporation, while I, although having a pretty good job, am certainly no "captain of industry."

When I was working as a freight handler at a railroad station in Iowa many years ago, one of my co-workers on the platform was a Negro, and a pretty smart young man. He, too, had about the same ability and inherent intelligence that I had. Today, he is still a freight handler while I have come several steps up the industrial ladder.

My studious college classmate, my Negro co-worker, and I probably all had about the same potential. I do not begrudge my college friend his success. He earned it. The Negro who worked with me in my younger days would have every right to begrudge me my success, or at least to hate the system that gave me my special privilege. He would know that he would not have been permitted to achieve my success, regardless of his efforts.

Question: Why do you fight racial discrimination? What's in it for you?

Answer: I fight it for the usual reasons, of course. Most liberals can glibly reel off motives for trying to eliminate prejudice and I am no exception. But we must be practical about these matters and concede that pleas for justice, democracy, and morality generally fall on deaf ears. Expediency, rather than ethics, seems to govern the actions of most of us.

Businessmen think of expediency when they refuse to serve Negroes in restaurants; then, later, it is often expediency which causes them to desegregate.

Politicians are thinking of expediency rather than morality when they exploit the race issue.

Preachers are thinking about expediency rather than ethics when they blandly ignore the fact that the country is boiling over with racial problems, and argue about whether creation only took seven calendar days or possibly a little longer. So let us talk about expediency.

I fight racial prejudice because I am sick, sick, sick of the whole business of race. I am sick of seeing pictures of teen-age and pre-teen-age Negro children being knocked down by high-pressure hoses, bitten by police dogs, and carted off to jails. I am sick of hearing otherwise fine and wholesome white teen-age children tell crude racial jokes. I am weary of seeing otherwise inept politicians keep getting elected by demagoguery. I'm fed up with hearing preachers perjure themselves and the message they bring just to appease a few racists in their congregations. I'm bone-tired of hearing our President and other national leaders insulted, condemned, and cursed for merely defending the Negro's constitutional rights.

I know the subject will continue to dominate conversations, thoughts, and actions just about every place I go until this battle is won. A lot of people, including many good friends of mine, give the impression that they think we could return to the customs we had a generation ago and that we could resegregate all the football, basketball, and baseball teams, the trains, the planes, and the buses, the libraries, the restaurants, the hotels and the parks, the schools and the shops. They really seem to believe that America can stand still, in human relations while the rest of the world moves on.

We liberals know better, but have difficulty, sometimes, persuading the recalcitrant. The analogy that has often been effective for me has to do with my fondness for the steam locomotive. The nostalgia I feel when I think of the lonesome wail of the mikado locomotive in the distance, and the staccato exhaust of the fast express must be similar to the memories some of my segregationist friends have of Uncle Tom. But I tell my segregationist friends that as badly as I hate to admit it, I know I can stand on the station platform from now until doomsday and never hear that deep-throated whistle again. Old No. 10's drivers will never flash in the sun again. The steam giant has done gone forever—and so has Uncle Tom.

So why torture ourselves with thoughts of what might be, but is not going to be? We know that sooner or later racial segregation in public places is going to disappear from the American scene, as far as I am concerned, the sooner the better. It seems obvious there will continue to be trouble until this is accomplished. Let's get on with the business of eliminating segregation and prejudice, so we can think of something else!

Chapter 13

THE HARVEST

Therefore said he unto them,
The harvest truly is great,
but the laborers are few . . .
                    —Luke 10:2

Although the road toward racial good will is not nearly so lonesome as it used to be, there is still much to be done. It is one thing to sit back and applaud the efforts of Negroes or other minorities. It is quite another thing to be willing to work and make personal sacrifices to help them. We need to remember what the young generation of Negroes have said to author Gordon Parks: "Some speak of well-intentioned whites: If they are sincere they will raise their voices above those of the racists."[1]

We need to make this willingness to raise our voices acceptable in a lot more places. It has long been possible for educators, scientists, writers, and journalists to speak out against racism even in regions where segregation has been *the* way of life. They usually have done their speaking in the friendly confines of the conference room, the community unity seminar, and in the university. But they *have* raised their voices. What we must do is make the denunciation of racism popular

[1] *Life*, August 16, 1963.

in the barber shop, the factory, the pool hall, the bar, and the church. We can struggle along with the race problems for another fifteen or twenty years, or we can be done with them in two or three. I think getting the matter settled justifies the enlistment of as many laborers as possible.

I sincerely hope the telling or our experiences will be of help to those who would like to do more than just observe. We have found that there is no substitute for hard work, and we have found that there is great power in the spoken word. There are words that can be very effective in the human rights struggle and if you feel, as my family and I do, the importance of getting Americans pulling together instead of calling each other names, then use these words. If you repeat them often enough, one day you will be surprised to hear the fellow who used to be an extreme segregationist remark, "Now I'm for segregation, but I'm not one of these extremists." And the man who used to be a moderate will say to you, "What can I do to help?" And the people who have been liberal all along will be saying, "Sure thing, let me get my checkbook."

Although I have stressed the tragic fact that organized religion has been a Johnny-come-lately in the struggle we speak of, I return to the subject of religion because of its great importance. One of the most important persons you can talk to about racial prejudice is your preacher.

When I felt completely frustrated about the racism that seemed to grip Little Rock a few years ago, I went to a minister to talk about it. I was surprised to find that he felt about as I did. Why he had said nothing about it from the pulpit is something only he can answer. But he did preach on prejudice shortly after our talk. The thing to remember is that most preachers know quite well that acts of prejudice are flagrant violation of many of God's commandments. But often the ministers hesitate to talk about the sin of race prejudice because they do not realize they have any support at all from their congregations. They will never realize it—unless you tell them!

When one member of a congregation decides to speak out, others will follow. If your preacher is against racial prejudice, and the congregation is for it, and you are against it, remember that because of the preacher's influence, you can become *a majority of one!*

You will find that the work you do in the field of human relations can produce great changes in your life. You will discover that your life can become satisfying, rewarding and meaningful. At least it will seem that way to those of you who were not, as we were not, used to much of anything out of the ordinary. We had the feeling that we were having a part in something very big, something very worthwhile and important.

When I first became active, in Little Rock, in opposition to race prejudice and in opposition to those who encourage prejudice, several good friends became quite apprehensive and told me that while they agreed with me in principle, they saw no reason why I should "stick my neck out." One good friend put it this way, "You'd better take a long look, down that 'lonesome road,' before you travel on."

I did take a long look, but continued down the road, I guess, because every time I tried to talk myself out of positive action, I seemed to recall Polonius' admonition to Laertes, "This above all: to thine own self be true, and it must follow as the night the day, thou cans't not then be false to any man."

A final word to those of you who may have been struggling with your consciences: Come on in, the waters of good will are just fine. And the road you have to take getting there won't be lonesome at all. You'll find it crowded with people from *all* parts of America who are beginning to see that when rights supposed to be inherent in citizenship are denied one group, then no one can be sure who might be next.

DEDICATION

Getting this book in print would not have been possible without the help of many people. The help and encouragement they provided enabled Carl and me to get our book about prejudice published in 1960. Most important, these people have motivated me, and I am sure have motivated many others, to work just a little harder in all areas of the human-rights struggle.

For this reason the names of the people to whom I dedicate this book should be of particular interest to all who want to help rid America to bigotry and hate. No doubt these same names will also be of particular interest to all of those who would prefer to retain bigotry and hate.

I list the names in no particular order, except the order in which I pulled their letters out of my filing cabinet.

1. DR. DAVID D. FOOTE

Dr. Foote is a Chicago dentist. He is eighty-four years of age and is still active in his profession. In 1918 Dr. Foote was licensed to practice dentistry in Vicksburg, Mississippi, the first Negro so privileged. As one of the leaders in the Negro community he was asked to assist in the sale of Liberty Bonds. It was urgent, the Negroes were told, to make the world safe for democracy.

Dr. Foote was one of three Negro professional men who were asked by the white leaders of Vicksburg to spearhead the drive for funds among Negroes. At a meeting about the matter, the group's leader, a Dr. Miller (a graduate of the University of Michigan), was asked the reason for the seeming reluctance on the part of Negroes to participate. Dr. Miller said flatly that his group thought democracy a very worthy goal, but that they would like to see a little more of it practiced in Mississippi.

In the days that followed, Dr. Foote went to Chicago on business. Dr. Miller was tarred and feathered and paraded through the streets of Vicksburg by a group of "vigilantes," and the third member of the group turned up in New Orleans. While in Chicago, Dr. Foote received the following telegram from a brother in Vicksburg:

"Prepare to live in Chicago; you cannot live here any longer."

When I visited Dr. Foote in Chicago forty-two years later, he told me this story. When he used the words, "You cannot live here any longer," I did not understand how this could be. But he had understood perfectly.

Dr. Foote managed to establish a dental practice in Chicago and has been very successful. But he has never stopped battling for civil rights. He has given generously whenever he thought his money could help fight injustice. On railroad trips back to the South through the years, Dr. Foote has consistently refused to be segregated whenever it could be avoided. At railroad stations he would stand out on the platform in any kind of weather rather than submit to the humiliation of being "Jim Crowed" into the colored waiting room.

In 1960 Dr. Foote read *This Is What We Found* and wrote me about it. Since then he has written me three or four times each week. Whenever he has run across a clipping or a new book he thought I could use, he has mailed it to me. The item in *Jet* magazine about Governor Faubus came to me from Dr. Foote.

I wish that I had retained all of Dr. Foote's communications. There would have been ample material in them for another book. I have saved several of his letters and close my tribute to him with a quote from one of them:

"I am thankful that so many more white men are showing they are the Negro's friend. They show they are on the side of fair play and justice. You do not have to be a 'nigger lover' to stand for fair play and Christianity. In my humble opinion, a Christian could take no other stand. As for others, I can only say, 'may God have mercy on their souls.'"

2. JOSEPH L. RAFT, program manager of Radio Free Europe

Mr. Raft held a fifteen-minute taped telephone interview with Carl, calling him out of his classroom at Central High for this purpose. This tape was used later in broadcasts to Iron Curtain countries. We were told that the knowledge a book such as ours could be, and was, written in Little Rock would be helpful in the fight against communism.

3. MRS. ELEANOR ROOSEVELT

Mrs. Roosevelt, even though ill, took time to write me several letters of encouragement. She devoted one of her syndicated columns to the work my family and I were trying to do.

4. OSCAR COHEN, program director for the Anti-Defamation League

For letters of encouragement, and for helping to make our book known.

5. DAVID BRINKLEY

For his helpful advice to me in a telephone conversation about how to find a publisher.

6. MARGARET LONG, author and columnist

For her very nice tribute to Carl and me in the Atlanta *Constitution.*

7. ARTHUR GOLDBERG

For a nice letter of encouragement and for his own devotion to the principle of equal justice under the law.

8. SENATORS DOUGLAS, SALTONSTALL, SYMINGTON, PROXMIRE, MILLER, WILLIAMS, KEFAUVER, DIRKSEN, and HUMPHREY

For their letters of encouragement and for their own efforts to secure equal rights for all Americans.

9. MRS. I. S. MCCLINTON

Mrs. McClinton is a blind Negro woman living in Little Rock. She has been very active in rehabilitation work for the blind. She managed to put herself through college after she became blind and after her three children were grown. *This Is What We Found* was read to her and she took on the rather large project of sending a copy of the book to each United States senator.

10. SENATOR HERMAN TALMADGE

For the very nice letter he wrote Mrs. McClinton thanking her for the book. She got letters from most of the liberal senators but was pleasantly surprised to hear from Senator Talmadge.

11. WINTHROP ROCKEFELLER

For his interest in what Carl and I wrote and for calling his friend Ralph McGill in a special effort to get what we had written published in the *Atlantic Monthly*.

12. BETTY FURNESS

For her helpfulness to me when I appeared on her television show and for her words of encouragement about my efforts in the field of human rights.

13. DR. BENJAMIN FINE, editor, North American Newspaper Alliance

For his letters of encouragement and for his efforts to help me find a publisher.

14. WILLIAM J. FALLIS, book editor, Broadman Press (of the Southern Baptist Convention)

For his letter of encouragement about my literary endeavors.

15. EDWARD R. MURROW, formerly of the United States Information Agency

For his letters of encouragement and his expressed interest in this book.

16. HARRY GOLDEN

Mr. Golden is very special. Aside from the fact he has given me so much encouragement and has written the introduction for this book, I have learned a great deal just by reading his books and his newspaper. I learned that in writing about bigotry and prejudice, one laugh is worth a thousand solemn pronouncements.

I wish there was some way I could adequately repay Mr. Golden. I have the feeling that if this book helps in any way to reduce the amount of racial prejudice and hate in America, this will be all the payment he wants.

In some of Harry Golden's writings he has mentioned instances of prejudice among Jews. He says that Jews displaying prejudice against other minority groups are not very convincing, but that you do find it occasionally.

I give you my solemn pledge, Harry, that if you will keep doing what you can to eliminate racial prejudice among Jews, I will keep working on the Baptists. How do you like this for a fifty-fifty proposition?

17. BROOKS HAYS, formerly Special Assistant to President Kennedy

For his letters and calls of encouragement and for his help in trying to find a publisher for the book Carl and I wrote. Most important, for his decision that he would rather be right than congressman.

18. LLOYD K. GARRISON, New York attorney

For letters of encouragement and offers of help.

19. ROBERT O. FERM, manager, Billy Graham Evangelistic Association

For his letters of encouragement.

20. REV. J. C. HERRIN, of the American Baptist Home Mission Board

For letters of encouragement and for the college scholarship grant he secured for Gloria Nelson, the colored girl we became friends with through the Arkansas Council on Human Relations' "Bridges across the Barriers" program.

21. JACKIE ROBINSON

For letters of encouragement and for his special role in breaking down the barriers.

22. HARRY ASHMORE, editor, Encyclopaedia Britannica (formerly editor of the *Arkansas Gazette*)

For his letters of encouragement and for his own willingness to stand, seemingly alone, when the going was really rough in 1957.

23. RICHARD KORNMEYER, head of the Book and Bible Division, Sunday School Board, Southern Baptist Convention

For letters of encouragement, and for his offer of help in trying to find a publisher for a book I had written.

24. KIVIE KAPLAN, Boston industrialist

For his many letters of encouragement; for telling others about my writing; and for other gestures of good will.

25. JULIUS SCHATZ, director, Community Service Bureau of the American Jewish Congress

For letters of encouragement and for making arrangements to place the manuscript for this book with Harold Ober Associates, literary agents.

26. JUSTINE WISE POLIER, Justice, Domestic Relations Court, New York City

For several letters of encouragement, and for speaking to others about my writing.

27. REV. S. RALPH HARLOW, author and professor emeritus of Smith College

For many letters of encouragement and for telling Kivie Kaplan about the book Carl and I wrote.

28. HODDING CARTER, editor, Greenville, Mississippi, *Delta Democrat Times*

For his encouragement and the hospitality he showed my wife and me when we visited in Greenville.

29. LILLIAN SMITH, Georgia author

For her help and advice about getting a book published.

30. MRS. ELLEN KILDUFF, housewife

When New Orleans was having its school troubles, Mrs. Kilduff attempted to give the school board $500,000 to meet their payroll, so the schools would not be forced to close.

Mrs. Kilduff has written me many letters of encouragement. She read the original manuscript for this book and made helpful suggestions.

In addition to all of these mentioned, there were many others who provided me with needed motivation. Included are a host of politicians who have tried to capitalize on social unrest. And I would not want to overlook the many writers of letters to such newspapers as the *Arkansas Democrat*, whose letters often start out with the theme, "Now I don't try to force my way into no country club, why do . . . ?"

DATE D'''